FORTUNES

OF

THE MOOR

TO OUR

GRANDCHILDREN

COURTNEY

AND

CONRAD

FORTUNES
OF
THE MOOR

by

Barbara and Carlton Molette

To order additional copies of this book, contact:
Xlibris
1-888-795-4274
www.Xlibris.com
Orders@Xlibris.com
741219

 ON THE COVER: Sankofa means go back to retrieve it. African people often use the image of a long necked bird looking to its rear to reinforce the idea that it is wise to look back and consider the past before moving forward in the present and into the future. Sankofas range stylistically from relatively realistic depictions to abstract symbols.

This image is reproduced from *African Design From Traditional Sources* by Geoffrey Williams, Dover Publications, Inc.

CONTENTS

SYNOPSIS

Shakespeare's *Othello* concludes as Desdemona's cousin Lodovico urges his uncle Gratiano to "seize upon the fortunes of the Moor." *Fortunes of The Moor*, once described in *The New York Times* as "a sequel to *Othello*," asks "What if, after Othello leaves to wage war against the Cypriots, Desdemona, disowned by her father, moves into a convent, discovers she is pregnant, and gives birth to a son?" After the Venetian victory in Cyprus under Othello's command, Desdemona leaves their infant son at the Venetian convent and joins Othello in Cyprus. After Desdemona's and Othello's tragic demise, both families learn the couple is survived by an infant son.

Conflict arises as each family seeks to claim the child and raise him as their own. Each family presumes its cultural identity, heritage, and rights of inheritance exceeds the other family's and asserts the right and the obligation to instill its values in and through this child with one Venetian parent and one African parent. Hassan, Othello's uncle, his wife, Elissa, and Othello's sister Somaia journey to Venice to claim the child and take him back to Africa. Brabantio, Desdemona's father, wants to raise his grandson as a Venetian. Each side defends its claim for custody of the child by asserting its right– its obligation– to determine the child's cultural identity, heritage and values.

But there is a third side. Gratiano and Lodovico, recognizing the infant son is the legitimate heir to Othello's fortunes, must remove him as an obstacle in order to purloin Othello's sizeable wealth. Othello's kinsmen learned that Othello is survived by a son because Gratiano sent Lodovico off to Africa to find and tell them. Gratiano's initial goal was to get the Moors to take the child but not the child's inheritance. Gratiano believed he could convince Brabantio to disavow his grandson with such innuendos as "What if the savage disposition of the father simmers in the son?" But, by the time Othello's family arrives in Venice, Gratiano has realized his innuendos about the child, whom neither has ever seen, will not convince Brabantio to abandon his only grandson. Brabantio's resolve to claim the child provokes Gratiano to gratify his greed by weaving a web of deceit, kidnapping, and murder. Gratiano then implements his plan by persuading Lodovico to do the dastardly deeds.

The story takes place in Venice in 1565 as wealthy locals seek to invest in and profit from the rapidly-growing Atlantic slave trade; but the play is set in Africa. Othello's African kinsmen and neighbors enter the stage with costumes and masks, welcome the audience and introduce the griot– the oral historian and story teller who is responsible for perpetuating and celebrating the history of Othello's African home. The griot pours a libation and begins to narrate the story of a family's voyage to Venice in search of the son born to the Venetian Desdemona and their kinsman Othello. The griot assumes the role of Hassan. Others assume the roles of Elissa, Somaia and the Venetian characters. Still others form a chorus of African townspeople who comment on the action as it unfolds.

In the African theatrical style known as abibigoro, actors may speak directly to the audience and masks may enable actors to portray more than one character. Hassan is both the story teller (griot) and the character from whose point of view the story is told. The play may use masks to represent characters and to transcend "racial" physiognomy by using "White" masks to portray Venetian characters, and "African" masks to portray Moors. The use of masks enables as few as eight actors to portray eleven characters.

The play is readily adaptable to thrust or arena stages and theatres with no fly system. Continuous action is essential and can be accomplished with scenery that eschews realistic depiction of various locales which require time for shifting scenery or properties. *Unit set, 125 minutes, 6 men, 5 women (with doubling– 4 men, 4 women).*

While Drama Critic Christopher Rawson's March 31, 2001 review in the *Pittsburgh Post-Gazette* (p. C-8) mostly focused (as it should) on Kuntu Repertory Theatre's production values, he said this about the script:

> "Fortunes of the Moor" (1995) operates on many levels–testing the claims of Othello's and Desdemona's relatives; exploring a clash between 17th-century cultures (Venetian commercialism and African communalism); indicting the racism of the church; and raising the larger issue of rights parental, familial, social and financial.
>
> The springboard is at the end of Shakespeare's play, where,... her kinsman, Lodovico, tells her paternal uncle, Gratiano, to "seize upon the fortunes of the Moor, for they succeed on you."
>
> Note that this disinherits Othello's own family. And how characteristic of a 17th-century Venetian (not to mention an Englishman) to think of booty even in the presence of tragedy! As a much-honored general, Othello's assets must be huge.
>
> Then the Molettes add one asset more: A baby, left by Desdemona at a Venetian convent.

CAST OF CHARACTERS

HASSAN– Othello's uncle, late 50's; wealthy merchant, quietly persuasive, not a warrior, so he need not appear larger or stronger than other men. He is the story teller (griot) and the character from whose point of view the story is told.

SOMAIA– Othello's sister, late 30's; zealously determined to raise Othello's son, takes herself very seriously.

ELISSA– married to Hassan for 30 years, late 40's; comfortable with her status.

GRATIANO– Brabantio's brother, late 40's; has no conscience, alternates from domineering and abusive to seemingly tender and attentive in his family relationships.

CRISTOFOLO– senator and merchant, late 50's; wealthy but miserly busybody.

BRABANTIO– Desdemona's father, late 50's; recovering from serious illness amid rumors of his death, senator. As the eldest son, he inherited the entirety of his father's fortune. His relatives are totally dependent on his largess.

LODOVICO– Brabantio's nephew, mid 30's; considers himself a ladies' man, wears the latest fashions, not very smart.

FRANCESCO– Gratiano's son, late 20's; has a moral compass, unlike his father whom he avoids, in part to escape his fathers's abusive behavior.

(MORE)

CAST OF CHARACTERS (continued)

BIANCA– Lodovico's courtesan, mid-30's; enjoys the dubious status and security Lodovico's social station provides.

SISTER ANNA– a nun, much older than Reverend Mother; her memory often fails her, loves caring for the children.

REVEREND MOTHER– head of the convent, mid 50's; fervently committed to her church, appears compassionate but tolerates no nonsense as manager of the convent.

Masks enable the play's eleven characters to be portrayed by as few as eight actors with doubling as indicated.

HASSAN, SOMAIA, ELISSA, GRATIANO and **REVEREND MOTHER** do not double.

The characters that may double are:

CRISTOFOLO may double as **BRABANTIO**

LODOVICO may double as **FRANCESCO**

BIANCA may double as **SISTER ANNA**

ACT ONE

SCENE ONE

PROLOGUE --- HASSAN's village in Africa.

TOWNSPEOPLE enter wearing or carrying
African masks. Some later become named
characters and the rest form a chorus. Sometimes
all speak in unison and at other times they speak
as three groups indicated as VOICES #1, #2, #3.

METAPHOR: During the prologue, an empty cradle
is revealed. The cradle remains throughout, using
lighting to increase or reduce the audience's
awareness of the cradle as appropriate.

TOWNSPEOPLE
Akwaaba!
*(The double A in akwaaba indicates the Ahhh sound
should be held for at least double the duration of a
normal English syllable.)*

HASSAN enters. HASSAN, as the GRIOT,
should recognize and speak to the audience.

HASSAN
(Speaks to the audience as GRIOT.)
Akwaaba!

VOICES #1
Akwaaba means you are welcome.

VOICES #2
We welcome you and we hope you enjoy the performance we
have prepared for you.

VOICES #3
As we begin, our Griot will pour a libation.

Lightning and thunder.

HASSAN
(As the GRIOT.)
Heaven shouts, earth trembles! O great God of all the
universe, you are strong, you are mighty. You fill every place
with your beauty. The whole earth is beneath you.
(Holds the vessel close to the ground and pours.)
I will tell the story of Hassan, Elissa, and Somaia, your humble
servants who traveled across the sea to a distant land called
Venice. When danger confronted them, they never lost sight
of their mission-- to cherish our children as the ancestors have
taught us.
(Holds the vessel close to the ground and pours.)
I beseech the ancestors to travel with us on this journey. Allow
those who hear my words to see the story as it unfolds. May
the ancestors receive these libations in the spirit in which we
offer them.
*(Holds the vessel close to the ground, pours, drinks
remaining liquid.)*
My friends, and neighbors, my brothers and my sisters, will
you inspire this chronicle with your participation?

TOWNSPEOPLE
Let our words cause every ear to hear the truth.

HASSAN
(Indicates "guests" are the audience.)
Will you enact my narrative so our guests will see, and know,
and remember the story as it actually took place?

TOWNSPEOPLE
Let our actions provoke each eye to see beyond the surface into
the depths of truth.

HASSAN

(As the GRIOT.)
I shall reveal a fascinating story in which avarice begets deceit
and intrigue begets murder. But first, I shall remind you of our
kinsman, Tarik. When he was just a boy, some evil men found
him alone, not far from this very place. These men brutally
attacked him and took him away before we knew he was in
danger. The vicious kidnappers shipped our kinsman to a
distant land called Venice and sold him as a slave. In keeping
with their custom, his captors refused to call him by the name
his family gave him. His captors gave him the name "Othello."

TOWNSPEOPLE

Othello.

HASSAN

As the boy they called Othello grew into manhood, his
prodigious bravery and courage won his freedom. As time
passed, his profound mind and military valor so amazed his
captors that they commissioned him commander of the whole
Venetian army. As we know, he married a Venetian whose
name was Desdemona.

TOWNSPEOPLE

Desdemona.

HASSAN

Desdemona's father was a man of great wealth and influence.
His name was Brabantio.

TOWNSPEOPLE

Brabantio.

HASSAN

And Brabantio so opposed his daughter's marriage that he
banished her from his home.

VOICES #1
A father cannot banish his own daughter!

VOICES #2
Our ancestors have taught us there is no wealth where there are
no children.

VOICES #3
When we are gone, what is left on earth to cause occasional
recollection that we were here?

VOICES #1
Do our good works inspire memorial?

VOICES #2
Our good works remain when we are gone, but only briefly.

VOICES #3
Immortality lies not in wealth or fame or power, but in our
children.

TOWNSPEOPLE
No pain is as great as dying without leaving a child behind.

HASSAN
Soon after his marriage, Tarik's military duties require him to
depart from Venice. Since Desdemona is no longer welcome in
her father's home, she takes refuge at a convent. The women
there are called sisters of their church. They keep nothing for
themselves except for bare necessity, and devote their lives to
offering a home and care and love to children abandoned by
some catastrophic circumstance. Thus, it comes to pass, a son
is born unto our kinsman as he leads Venetian forces into battle
against the Ottomans.

TOWNSPEOPLE
Unto our kinsman, a son is born!

HASSAN

After Tarik leads the Venetians to victory, he remains in
Cyprus as military governor. Desdemona joins Tarik and
leaves their son in the care and protection of the sisters of the
convent. Later, Tarik's trusted assistant, a soldier named Iago,
betrays Tarik and murders both Tarik and Desdemona as they
sleep. Iago even murders his own wife when she threatens to
reveal his colossal evil.

TOWNSPEOPLE

After Desdemona and Tarik are gone, who is responsible for
the child? Who will teach him to wash his hands, so he can eat
with the elders?

ELISSA & SOMAIA

(In unison.)

We have prepared a place for him in our village. We will teach
him who he is, and who he can become.

HASSAN

Our story continues as friends and family wish Hassan, Elissa,
and Somaia a safe and successful voyage to the distant land
called Venice to claim our kinsman, the child of Tarik and
Desdemona.

> Music and dancing as the GRIOT becomes
> HASSAN and some TOWNSPEOPLE become,
> and dance as Venetians. Others continue to dance
> as Africans. As music fades, **CROSSFADE to...**

SCENE TWO

HASSAN's ship

The ship approaches Venice at daybreak. Most of what is said in this scene is spoken directly to the audience.

HASSAN
We traveled across the sea and into the tranquil waters of the Venetian harbor. The wind and weather favored our voyage. Somaia provided our only excitement when she offered our crew instructions in the art of sailing.

SOMAIA
I only asked if we could go a bit faster.

HASSAN
Our safe arrival beckoned both relief and revelry. Although we're aliens here, our purposes will not succumb to fear.

SOMAIA
So, this is Venice.

ELISSA
I cannot wait to get off this vessel.

HASSAN
(To ELISSA, making fun of her impatience.)
You cannot get off the vessel until the vessel reaches the pier.

SOMAIA
(To HASSAN.)
What if these Venetians continue to blame Tarik?

HASSAN
(To SOMAIA.)
We cannot restore Tarik's esteem among Venetians by
reminding them no proof supports the rumor that he murdered
Desdemona. And we need no assurance of his innocence.

SOMAIA
(Mostly to the audience.)
We treated Lodovico as a member of our family because he is
Desdemona's cousin. In return, he laughed at our customs and
called us primitive.

ELISSA
Beautiful clothes do not cover ugly manners.

SOMAIA
Does the city always appear so devoid of color?

HASSAN
The clouds make everything look gray.

SOMAIA
Yet, my joy increases as each moment moves us closer to our
aspiration.

ELISSA
(To SOMAIA.)
We cannot allow these clouds to suffocate our spirits.
(To the audience.)
But, I hope we soon find refuge from this awful weather.

SOMAIA
Anticipation of this happiness diminishes my residue of pain.
Each time, I felt the joy of a baby moving inside my body-- my
husband's pride puffed up like the swelling of my belly as he
felt the baby move inside me and we celebrated our good
fortune. Each time, our joy was crushed as I tried to push my
(MORE)

SOMAIA (Continued)

breath into my baby's breathless body. My first baby came lifeless from my womb, but my hope persisted. When my second infant never whimpered, my hopes were shattered. After my third child... I knew no life would ever come from here. Have the ancestors forsaken me?

ELISSA

(To SOMAIA.)

The ancestors have not abandoned you, Somaia. I have heard them whispering "Somaia's faith will soon be rewarded."

SOMAIA

(To the audience.)

How can anyone raise children in this place?

ELISSA

My husband tells us Venice is celebrated for its charm and beauty. Where do they hide these attributes?

HASSAN

(To ELISSA.)

Your husband has told you many times that Venice is far nobler in the telling than in actuality.

(The rest is mostly to the audience.)

The city is overcrowded, but the world hears of bustling businesses, magnificent buildings, and boundless variety. Transportation is troublesome, but we are only told of picturesque canals. Cathedrals abound, but the people are not pious. Markets are large and lavish, but they have nothing we cannot get at home for a more reasonable price. And while we're here, we must be ever vigilant. Venetians cloak their treachery and greed in cool detachment, and we have no way of knowing who among them is a slaver.

HASSAN looks toward the city through his telescope. **CROSSFADE to...**

SCENE THREE

A pier in Venice at daybreak.

GRATIANO looks through his telescope for
approaching ships, so he fails to notice
CRISTOFOLO approach.

CRISTOFOLO
Signior Gratiano? Signior Gratiano!

GRATIANO
(He recognizes CRISTOFOLO with feigned enthusiasm.)
Greetings, Signior Cristofolo!

CRISTOFOLO
What brings you here to the docks? Are you engaged in some
shipping enterprise?

GRATIANO
My only interest in shipping is the investment I hope to make
with you. My nephew, Lodovico, is aboard the ship that now
draws near.

CRISTOFOLO
The time draws near when we must have your investment.

GRATIANO
I'll deliver the sum I promised by the midday meal tomorrow.

CRISTOFOLO
This opportunity is only available to you because you are
Senator Brabantio's brother. Although he is my friend, and I
respect his judgment, Brabantio stubbornly contends these
Moorish creatures are altogether human despite opinions to the
contrary from our most distinguished clergymen and scholars.
After his only daughter was murdered by one of the beasts, one
(MORE)

CRISTOFOLO (Continued)

would think he would have learned. I would never permit my daughter to make acquaintance with a Moor.

GRATIANO

I did not know you had a daughter.

CRISTOFOLO
(Ignores because he has no daughter.)

When Othello's ferocity against the Ottomans met with nearly universal praise, I expressed the view that Venetian victory might have come at a price too dear. I would not say this except you are Brabantio's brother, and one who loves him dearly, as do I. The town is bursting with allegations of a son sired by the Moor. But, I have ignored the rumors.

GRATIANO

I am blessed by your offer to participate in such a lucrative enterprise.

CRISTOFOLO
(Routinely presents his plan to attract investors, complete with documentary evidence.)

Our trickle of an investment will turn into a torrent of riches if we abandon hesitation. His Holy Eminence has instructed the Bank of Saint George to provide whatever we require to employ a Portuguese captain and crew to sail our vessel.

GRATIANO

Would not our trust be better placed among our own Venetian sailors?

CRISTOFOLO

The Portuguese excel at shipping slaves. Our captain knows how to tightly pack a ship to attain the maximum cargo. Allowing for losses from rationing food and water and stern
(MORE)

CRISTOFOLO (Continued)
security generates more income than efforts to keep all the
slaves alive with more abundant food and space.

GRATIANO
How many slaves can we afford to lose?

CRISTOFOLO
We need deliver only 400 of the 800 slaves we ship to clear a
handsome profit. A slave who attempts escape must be killed
and the body displayed for the remaining cargo. The sight and
smell of a few dead bodies provide the strongest deterrent to
further acts of violence. We make an effort to deliver every
slave we put on board, but losses are inevitable. Those who
disagree do not recognize our purpose which is financial gain.

GRATIANO
I'll use my wealth to buy great works of art for Venice. My
patronage will cause our city to be known throughout the world
for its unsurpassed refinement.

CRISTOFOLO
The world is available for our benefit and control. But, we
must hasten to harvest the vast resources from these dark and
pagan places.

GRATIANO
Your confidence in this Portuguese captain inspires me to
move quickly.

CRISTOFOLO
His present voyage takes him to the West Indies where he'll
sell his cargo of slaves and purchase sugar cane and tobacco
bound for England. The English demand a monstrous tariff on
tobacco, but our captain is quite successful at evading their
scrutiny.

GRATIANO
Smuggling?

> LODOVICO shouts from offstage as he enters.

LODOVICO
Uncle Gratiano!

GRATIANO
Welcome home, Lodovico!

LODOVICO
The countenance of Venice shines more brightly this day than any I have seen.

> Drumming is heard in the distance as the Moors approach.

GRATIANO
Contrast the fineness of Venice with the coarseness of your Moorish visitations in weeks ahead. For now, let us hurry
(Emphasis to mean: CRISTOFOLO must not hear this!)
home so you can tell me of your mission in privacy.

LODOVICO
(Fails to get the point.)
I found Othello's father and told him...

GRATIANO
(Interrupts before LODOVICO reveals more.)
Lodovico, you remember our dear friend, Signior Cristofolo?

LODOVICO
(Still fails to get the point.)
Greetings, Signior Cristofolo.

CRISTOFOLO

What is that ship of alien configuration?

LODOVICO

Othello's uncle comes to claim his heir and return with him to
Africa.

CRISTOFOLO
(Eager to spread the gossip.)
Urgent business obliges me to forsake your gracious company.

CRISTOFOLO exits.

GRATIANO

You may depend upon my promise.
(After CRISTOFOLO is gone.)
Your welcome diminishes as rapidly as a fool's wealth.
Cristofolo is off to spread the scandal of Desdemona's baby
blackamoor.

LODOVICO

A gossip monger's words cannot deter our quest. Othello's
fortune still belongs to us!

GRATIANO

Before you squander a fortune you have yet to obtain...

LODOVICO

How is Uncle Brabantio?

GRATIANO

He knows about the child because you cannot hold your
tongue. If he claims the little savage...

LODOVICO

...poverty will enlist us in its ranks.

GRATIANO

I try to make Brabantio despise the child by happily
proclaiming he bears a close resemblance to the savage Moor.
I compliment the baby's wooly hair, thick lips, broad nose, and
ebony hue.

LODOVICO

In truth, does the boy resemble Othello?

GRATIANO

In truth I do not know, nor does it matter. The baby's
countenance is a weapon for Brabantio to draw upon himself.
He'll see whatever we convince him he sees.

LODOVICO

An excellent strategy.

GRATIANO

The sordid circumstance of the darksome baby's birth does not
decrease my brother's joy. He commands me to procure the
child on his behalf and says he'll raise the little bastard as his
heir.

LODOVICO

...leaving us with no inheritance!

GRATIANO

Drop by drop, my venom deadens his delight. I persuaded him
the Reverend Mother sent a message to Othello's kinsmen
asking if they wish to claim the child.

LODOVICO

You make your brother your fool!

GRATIANO

My fool provided money to purchase a magistrate's opinion.
Naturally, I kept most of it, but I paid enough to get a ruling
(MORE)

GRATIANO (Continued)

that keeps Brabantio from seizing Antonio. The nuns at the convent call the little savage "Antonio."

LODOVICO

Never again will we be forced to grovel at Brabantio's feet like beggars. While I was away, some personal business
(Starts to exit.)
has gone unattended...

GRATIANO

You call it business? Your shameful affair with a Contessa whose years outnumber your own mother's? If you persuade her to give you money, I suppose that is business.

LODOVICO

The Moors approach.

GRATIANO

But then, you give the Contessa's funds to Bianca, whose business is to gratify your libertine pleasure. Do not allow your rakish appetites to circumvent our purpose.

HASSAN, ELISSA, and SOMAIA, enter.

LODOVICO
(Interrupts GRATIANO to change the subject.)
Signior Hassan! Welcome to Venice!

GRATIANO

I am Gratiano, uncle to Lodovico and the fair Desdemona.

HASSAN
(Slightly bowing)
Peace be with you, Signior Gratiano. I am Hassan ben Akbar.

GRATIANO
Welcome Signior Hassan.

HASSAN
This is my wife, Elissa, and my sister's daughter, Somaia.

GRATIANO
Welcome, ladies. I am steadfast in support of your desire to claim your rightful heir, return to your homeland, and nurture the child in the ways of his father.

HASSAN
I am pleased to hear your sentiments, but where is the father of the woman my kinsman chose to be his wife? Why does he not welcome me?

GRATIANO
As I am an honest and forthright man, I must confess my brother does not support your purpose. But, my assistance guarantees you will achieve your goal. And why have you come to Venice instead of Othello's father?

HASSAN
I am the mother's brother, and our custom places that responsibility on me. Our custom further assigns the tasks of care and keeping of the child to his sister, Somaia.

SOMAIA
It is my duty and pleasure to raise my brother's child as though he were my own.

GRATIANO
Othello's child is fortunate to have a loving mother.

HASSAN
The name "Othello" was given to my kinsman by men who captured him and sold him as a slave. His father named him
(MORE)

HASSAN (Continued)
Tarik, in tribute to the African general who conquered Spain.
His soldiers named a place in Spain "Tarik's mountain." In our
language, the place is called "Gebel Tarik;" the Christians call
the place "Gibraltar."

GRATIANO
Othello never told us he had another name.

HASSAN
Your countrymen often give a Christian name to persons who
come from distant lands with names you find difficult to
pronounce.

GRATIANO
We loved your nephew and considered him Venetian.

HASSAN
Wood may remain in water for many years, but it will never
become a crocodile.

GRATIANO
        (Does not get the point.)
We intended him no harm or disrespect.

HASSAN
Our people say "It does not matter what people call you. What
matters is what you answer to." Tarik chose to answer to the
name "Othello" while in Venice. I honored his decisions, even
though I sometimes disagreed. Despite his choice to use his
military genius for the benefit of Venice, I loved Tarik as
though he were my son. And I will cherish his son as if he
were my own.

GRATIANO

Among my countrymen and yours, the younger generation
permits the heart to make determinations better made by
rational temperament.

HASSAN

Cactus is bitter only to those who taste it.
    (GRATIANO does not get this either.)
I look forward to conversing at greater length. But my first
concern is to see the child who is my heir.

GRATIANO

He is with some sisters of our church who cherish and protect
children who have been rebuked by fate, despite their
innocence. This evening, Lodovico and I will join you for
supper. I have arranged accommodations at the inn across the
square from the clock tower. When the clock strikes three, I
will direct you to the convent where the child is kept.

HASSAN

We'll tarry here until the crew collects our baggage.

LODOVICO

Farewell one and all.

LODOVICO exits hurriedly.

GRATIANO

I bid you farewell. Until three o'clock. Signior Hassan.
Ladies.

GRATIANO exits.

HASSAN

Observe the deceit of which these infidels are capable.

SOMAIA
(Imitates GRATIANO.)
"I am an honest and forthright man." This Gratiano smiles with
his teeth, but not with his heart.

ELISSA
But he is not as thin of thought as Lodovico.

HASSAN
These people have no sense of hospitality. I could not fail to
welcome Desdemona's father to my home.

ELISSA
I hope this foul odor is not everywhere.

SOMAIA
How could Tarik abide this place?

ELISSA
When one is in love, a cliff becomes a meadow.

SOMAIA
When I urged Tarik to leave this place, he spoke not of love
but of his fortune and celebrity.

ELISSA
Tarik exhibited no desire for wealth and adoration before his
capture and enslavement.

SOMAIA
No sister could love a brother more than I loved Tarik, but
these Venetians transformed him into one of them. His captors
gave him praise and wealth for the battles he won on their
behalf. He so cherished their gifts that he came to value their
well-being more than his own.

HASSAN

Chains that bind the body can be broken; but a captive mind requires neither cage nor watchman to invoke submissive servitude.

ELISSA

Tarik felt compassion for these people so constrained by fear that they they required his courage in absence of their own.

SOMAIA

Has courage so abandoned Venice that it must be imported?

HASSAN

If I had been with him when he desperately needed help, or enticed him more vigorously to come home...

ELISSA

You do not deserve this burden.

SOMAIA

You provided sage counsel for Tarik at every opportunity. He chose to remain in Venice.

HASSAN

Home affairs should not be discussed in a public place. Let us find our accommodations.

All exit. **CROSSFADE to...**

SCENE FOUR

Outside the convent, morning.

LODOVICO and BIANCA embrace as BIANCA seeks to heighten LODOVICO's desires so she can obtain funds. Repeatedly, LODOVICO nearly succumbs to his passions, but each time, he reluctantly reminds himself that he must not let his appetites circumvent his purpose.

LODOVICO
Not now, Bianca. Othello's kinsmen wait impatiently.

BIANCA
What gives these Moors the luxury of impatience? For three vacant months I waited virtuously for your return.

LODOVICO
This abstinence is at least as difficult for me. Holding firmly to my plan stiffens our cause. The Moors want Antonio to spend the evening with them so they can depart on tomorrow's first occasion. Achievement of their goal swells my purse. Have the blessed sisters prepare him for departure while I lead the dark procession here.

BIANCA
The Reverend Mother will demand assurance of legitimate prerogative.

LODOVICO
I'll solemnly certify, as sure as I am Desdemona's cousin, these Moors are Othello's kinsmen and they embrace this baby as Othello's rightful heir.

BIANCA
If the Reverend Mother learns Othello's kinsmen are not
Christian, she may not consider assignment of the child to
them.

LODOVICO
The Moorish women dress remarkably like our nuns. And so,
I'll tell the Reverend Mother these women of Othello's clan are
nuns themselves-- members of a far-off eastern order...

BIANCA
Do not trifle with the Reverend Mother. She will confound
your plans if you give her cause to doubt your honesty.

LODOVICO
You do not appreciate my wit. Only my humor has diminished
from lack of use. My craving is beyond...
        (He overcomes his urges.)
But only after little Antonio is safely on his way.

BIANCA
The blessed sisters adore the child and would obtain
contentment from raising him themselves.

LODOVICO
Do the sisters crave Antonio's fortune?

BIANCA
Of course not. The reverend sisters are sworn to poverty.

LODOVICO
And yet you extol their good judgment?

BIANCA
The Reverend Mother hungers for some excuse to keep the
child. And the church will support whatever she decides. If
(MORE)

BIANCA (Continued)
your plan softens, your promise to provide for me may
dwindle.

LODOVICO
Have I fulfilled my promises thus far?

BIANCA
You have been good to me, Lodovico. Your generous attention
and endowment furnish comfort and diversion. Moreover, I
admire the provider much, much more than your gifts. Others
could provide such gifts, but only you...

LODOVICO
What gifts have you accepted while I was away?

BIANCA
(Leans down so Lodovico sees inside her bodice.)
I wear the necklace you gave me under my bodice, close to my
heart to remind me of my commitment to you.

LODOVICO
You did not answer my question.

BIANCA
I have done nothing to arouse your suspicions.

LODOVICO
You arouse more than my suspicions, Bianca.
    (Aside.)
I must not be ruled by urges of the flesh until the Moorish baby
is away.

BIANCA
(Leads him to a bench, he resists-- weakly.)
I cannot restrain my excitement. Although civility goes
wanting in my demeanor, you must never doubt my honesty.

LODOVICO

My reliance on your honesty is evident. You informed me
Desdemona visited this convent to conceal her baby's birth.
With Desdemona dead and the nuns sworn to secrecy, only
your word confirms a child was born to Desdemona and
Othello. Surrendering to your trust, I divulged your testimony
to my family and Othello's. Now, each family covets the child
for its own purposes. Yet, none of us have the leanest evidence
of the child's identity except for your assurance.

BIANCA

I am as worthy of your trust as you are deserving of my
unswerving faithfulness. I've planned a meal and other
pleasantries to celebrate your return.

LODOVICO

I must dine with Othello's kinsmen.

BIANCA
(Her gesture asks for money.)
But some of the delights I want you to enjoy must be purchased
from the market.

LODOVICO

I long for your delights; but the Moors will be offended if their
sense of hospitality is breached.

BIANCA

The emptiness left unfilled by your absence must be...

LODOVICO
(His will power diminishes.)
At the first possible moment, I shall quit the dusky diners.

BIANCA

My passions have been restrained much, much, much too long.

LODOVICO

My impatience to culminate these months of deprivation expands with every moment. I must go before I violate decorum on this sacred site.

BIANCA
(Her gesture again asks for money.)
Will you supply the succulent delights I plan for you?

LODOVICO

I'll soon return with wherewithal to satisfy whatever scarcities you have encountered.

LODOVICO exits. BIANCA blows a kiss.
CROSSFADE to...

SCENE FIVE

The inn, quarters of HASSAN's party, morning.

HASSAN, ELISSA, and SOMAIA enter.

SOMAIA
I wonder if their homes are bleak and stagnant like this inn.

ELISSA
At least our quarters here do not rise and fall beneath us as the
vessel did at sea. I cherish this momentary rest on solid earth.

SOMAIA
Why do we not stay at Tarik's apartment? Are his lodgings
not esteemed as the most elegant in the city?

HASSAN
I intend to sell all of Tarik's Venetian properties in order to
insure financial independence for his son.

SOMAIA
Everything?

HASSAN
His apartment, his office, his villa by the sea, the olive groves
and vineyards, his investments at the Saint George Bank.

ELISSA
There must be some remedy for this moldy odor.

SOMAIA
Perhaps we could send to our vessel for some scented oils from
Egypt.

HASSAN

Everything in Venice is damp and moldy-- even Tarik's apartment, but I sympathize with your vexation.

ELISSA

How can you dismiss this awful stench as mere vexation?

SOMAIA

Tarik must have been miserable here.

ELISSA

He always had a talent for transforming things to his advantage, even as a child. Remember how he convinced all the boys in the village...

SOMAIA

I've heard the story many times before. How could I forget? Tarik devised a schedule so two or three boys would watch over all the goats so the others could go off and play.

ELISSA

But, since Tarik organized the schedule,

ELISSA & SOMAIA

(In unison.)
He never had to watch the goats.

HASSAN

Tarik did not go off and play. He practiced the skills his elders expected him to master in order to be accepted into the society of warriors.

SOMAIA

I have seen this "practice" as you call it. It looks like play to me.

ELISSA

I still marvel at his persuasiveness at such an early age. I knew
he would become an eloquent speaker.

SOMAIA

In your eyes, Tarik was perfect at everything.

ELISSA

Not everything. I wish Tarik had not told the children stories
about men whose heads grow beneath their shoulders and
people who eat human flesh.

SOMAIA

He learned those awful stories from the Venetians. Their
pleasure in frightening little children should not surprise us.

ELISSA

Somaia, you must be more tolerant.

SOMAIA

They wave a pot of smoking embers to cast out demons from
their place of worship-- and yet they call us heathen.

ELISSA

No doubt the stories we hear about these people contain
embellishments.

SOMAIA

They live in buildings made of stones that swallow the sun's
warmth. The stony chill invades their souls and spawns
conduct as cold and as hard as their dwellings.

ELISSA

At least the tales Tarik learned from the infidels were shorter
than the stories Hassan tells...

HASSAN

To forget one's ancestors is to be a tree without roots. Our history must be remembered and respected.

ELISSA

Hassan takes nearly as long to narrate history as it took for it to originally transpire.

SOMAIA

We must return with tributes worthy of my baby's homecoming.

ELISSA

The child needs no wealth beyond his living riches.

HASSAN

Living riches? The child never saw his father.

ELISSA

Living riches indeed. My grandchildren, four aunts and a grandmother who'll dote on him and cherish every breath, five uncles and a grandfather to guide his feet along the path to manhood.

HASSAN

He deserves his father's fortune and I will see that he gets it. We must be ready to sail as soon as our vessel has provisions and the weather favors our departure.

ELISSA

Surely we have time to visit their markets.

HASSAN

You say living riches will suffice, but delight in purchasing foreign merchandise for an infant.

ELISSA

The process of acquiring the thing is more fun than having the thing. And one more glass bottle or piece of tapestry will not force you to sleep out-of-doors.

HASSAN

When we stop in Tunis to replenish our supplies and sell whatever leather goods remain, you may spend as much time in their markets as you like. If you do not find enough to satisfy you there, we'll stop again in Algiers.

ELISSA

After all our years together, you know I can live without Venetian trinkets.

> ELISSA and HASSAN show affection as a couple married for several decades.

HASSAN

I need to occupy the time before the banks close for the midday meal to secure Tarik's estate.

SOMAIA

I noticed a little shop just across the canal. You can put your bargaining skills to good...

> SOMAIA exhibits a desire to exit.

ELISSA

We must obtain proper gifts for such a grand occasion as our baby's naming ceremony. While you handle your chores at the bank we can fetch the child and...

HASSAN

My uneasiness reflects concern for the baby's protection and our own. Did you notice the hostile stares we encountered as we arrived at the inn?

ELISSA

Their stares appear more curious than hostile. But even so, do hostile stares prove they intend to do us harm?

SOMAIA

Venetian morality offers no protection, but their cowardice provides a bit of solace.

HASSAN

I have repeatedly told you we provide our only protection here. I have even warned the members of our crew not to venture out alone.

ELISSA

We'll just take a look at what they have in the little shop across...

As ELISSA and SOMAIA exit.

HASSAN

Have at least two of our men accompany you.

HASSAN crosses out of the inn.

HASSAN (Continued)
(To the audience as GRIOT.)
While Elissa and Somaia allegedly went shopping, I began the tedious task of looking after Tarik's estate. So I contributed no excitement to the story for the remainder of the morning. Good people are often fascinated by evil deeds and the people who perpetrate them, so the story's focus shifts to Brabantio's home where Gratiano's avarice continues to foment extraordinary treachery. Long ago, a wise man said, "The ruin of a nation begins in the homes of its people."

CROSSFADE TO...

SCENE SIX

BRABANTIO's home, midday.

BRABANTIO and GRATIANO are present.

BRABANTIO
*(Pours himself a glass of wine without offering
   GRATIANO any.)*
Damnable petty bureaucrats!

GRATIANO
These minions envy your wealth and station.

BRABANTIO
Little Antonio is my only legacy.

GRATIANO
Little Antonio will grow up to be Antonio the Moor.

BRABANTIO
I have no other option to assure continuation of my blood.

GRATIANO
Continuation of your blood at what expense?

BRABANTIO
No expense appears too great for you so long as you disburse
the money from my purse.

GRATIANO
Everything I do is for your benefit.

BRABANTIO
For my benefit, and never for my money?

GRATIANO
Spiteful words destroy a brother as readily as a daughter.

BRABANTIO
What do you mean?

GRATIANO
I do not wish to...

BRABANTIO
You insinuate some spiteful words of mine destroyed my
daughter.

GRATIANO
You were justly angered when Desdemona deceived you. And
so you told the Moor, "As Desdemona deceived her father, she
will deceive her husband."

BRABANTIO
I was beguiled by Othello's valor and that matchless quality
which made men willingly follow him into battle.

GRATIANO
I pray the child inherits these enviable qualities without the
Moor's brutality.

BRABANTIO
I pray your fearful omens evaporate as fog in sunlight.

GRATIANO
I pray that you realize the baby's Moorish breeding prohibits a
refined life in Venice.

BRABANTIO
I would readily relinquish my resolve to keep Antonio if
another option assured continuation of my blood. Both your
(MORE)

BRABANTIO (Continued)
own son Francesco, and our nephew Lodovico regard you as
their father.

GRATIANO
I claim no son except for Lodovico.

BRABANTIO
You prefer Lodovico above your own son because Lodovico
accommodates your wishes without question or hesitation.

GRATIANO
How can I regard Francesco as my son when he publicly
accuses me of some unnamed treachery?

BRABANTIO
Francesco is much brighter than Lodovico. But, Lodovico's
blind indulgence renders you oblivious to his blundering.

GRATIANO
I know about Lodovico's exploits with the ladies.

BRABANTIO
"Ladies" you call them? I am told one of them is old enough to
be his mother and another entices travelers from their gondolas
at the Ponte delle Tette.

GRATIANO
His loyalty far outweighs his youthful indiscretion.

BRABANTIO
Lodovico's head does not quite fill his hat.

LODOVICO enters.

LODOVICO
Good afternoon, dear Uncle!

BRABANTIO
I see you survived the savages and their primitive surroundings. Welcome home to cultivated Venice.

LODOVICO
These Moors have no respect for privacy or property. I could never get a moment's solitude. Their quarters mix and mingle so several kinsmen share property without regard for rightful ownership. I could never specify who or what belonged to whom, or which adults were parents to which children. All the men call each other brother, but they do not share the same mother. The place was teeming with children. These Africans are incessant breeders.

GRATIANO
Their sable skins and coarser features prove their natures are more primitive than ours; but I contend it is the warmth of their climate that causes them to breed so rapidly. Our cooler climes encourage industrious activity, while their climate stirs the heat of their loins. With passion quenched, they have no motivation to pursue the more productive arts that make us civilized. We must not blame the dusky primitives. Cultivated Christians must help them overcome the baseness of their natures.

BRABANTIO
Save the stories of wild barbarians and their dark mysterious land. I only want to know if you convinced Othello's family to abandon any scheme to remove Antonio from my protection.

> LODOVICO does not know what to say, so he looks to GRATIANO.

GRATIANO
We know the Reverend Mother at the convent where Antonio resides sent a messenger inviting Othello's kin to claim the child.

BRABANTIO

She sent no messenger to encourage me. A woman should not
have authority to make decisions of such enormity.

GRATIANO

Othello's right of inheritance remains unblemished since the
Governor made him a full Venetian citizen, and his marriage
was sanctioned by the church. So the Reverend Mother can
dismiss our request for custody without consideration or
concern.

BRABANTIO

What could possess a Reverend Mother of the church to favor
these heathens over me?

LODOVICO

The Reverend Mother would not dare oppose your wishes.

BRABANTIO

And yet she does! The woman has taken leave of her senses.
First, the petty bureaucrats, then the Reverend Mother, and now
these Moors! Fools, women, and savages! None of them can
tell me what decision I should make. I will raise little Antonio
as my grandson.

GRATIANO

What if the savage disposition of the father simmers in the son?

BRABANTIO

The swaddling has been gifted with noble blood. That legacy
will raise his esteem in the eyes of men. I will devote the time
I have remaining to help Antonio overcome the unfortunate
portion of his heritage. I have been told on good authority the
infant does not resemble the dusky warrior.

GRATIANO

One sister says the child is the image of Desdemona while others tell me he is as dark and coarse of countenance as Othello.

BRABANTIO

I have been told the child resembles me.

LODOVICO

They wish to see the child as soon as possible.

BRABANTIO

How dare they come to Venice knowing Othello murdered my daughter?

LODOVICO

Persistent rumors contend Iago murdered Desdemona and Othello. And, when Iago's wife began to speak the truth, he slit her throat as well. Naturally, the Moors believe the version that favors their kinsman.

BRABANTIO

These Moors will never gaze upon my daughter's child!

LODOVICO

A visit to the convent has already been arranged.

GRATIANO

Arrangements can be undone.

BRABANTIO

What if they try to kidnap little Antonio?

LODOVICO

You must not worry, Uncle...

BRABANTIO

I'll worry until my wishes meet no challenge! What did you
tell them?

LODOVICO

I spoke with great sincerity on your behalf.

BRABANTIO

How did you make the case?

LODOVICO

I said they have no proof Othello is the father.

BRABANTIO

Are we so destitute of strategy that our best argument defiles
my daughter's reputation?

GRATIANO

These Moors are simple-minded people. You can persuade
them a rooster lays eggs. I'll arrange a meeting...

BRABANTIO

I will not meet with him. My birthright entitles me to raise this
child and control Othello's fortune as my own.

GRATIANO

Antonio's dark complexion and broad features are sure to grow
more prominent as the years increase.

LODOVICO

His father's blood pollutes our lineage.

GRATIANO

Antonio is a Moor, and a Moor should be raised by barbarians.

BRABANTIO

I would rather see him dead.

GRATIANO
Are you certain it serves your interests to raise this child as a
Venetian nobleman?

BRABANTIO
My interests will be served when my grandson is here with me
and I control Othello's fortune.

GRATIANO
Then, I will kidnap the child.

BRABANTIO
I cannot sanction kidnapping.

LODOVICO
Justice favors your intent.

BRABANTIO
After my near-fatal illness and Desdemona's brutal murder, I
lost all impetus to live. Antonio has resurrected me. I will not
allow this Moor to steal my legacy. Do what you must without
informing me of the particulars.

> After BRABANTIO exits, GRATIANO pours a
> glass of wine.

GRATIANO
I enjoyed a surprisingly swift reduction in my expenses while
you were too far away to siphon off my funds.

LODOVICO
I have been loyal to you.

GRATIANO
Apparently, the resources I willingly provide do not suffice to
satisfy your lavish appetites.

LODOVICO
I do not deserve...

GRATIANO
Do not insult me with further protestations.

LODOVICO
(As he pours a glass of wine.)
You exaggerate my indulgences.

GRATIANO
You drink to excess. You gamble beyond your means. You prance about the city in expensive clothes arousing ladies to sigh and say "What a handsome sight is Lodovico." Being well dressed does not prevent one from being poor. Only one eventuality assures our prosperity-- completion of the Moorish heir's demise.

LODOVICO
What do you mean demise?

GRATIANO
I mean the child must die.

LODOVICO
Why can't we follow our original plan? I sacrificed these many months away from Venice finding Othello's family and arranging to send the child away in the care of the Moors.

GRATIANO
That plan presumed Brabantio could be persuaded to abandon the child just as he abandoned Desdemona. But even you can see Brabantio cannot be diverted from his wish. And so, the child must die. Further, you must not be diverted by debauchery until the deed is done.

LODOVICO

Why not kidnap the baby and sell him into slavery? You say
all of them are better off as slaves.

GRATIANO

Risk to us outweighs your charitable bent.

LODOVICO

The child's Moorish features commend it readily to such a fate.

GRATIANO

The child's identity would certainly become known among the
slavers. Brabantio would offer a ransom exceeding the value
of the child as a slave. A slaver would never honor a promise
over a profit. No course of action leads to our advantage
except to kill the child.

LODOVICO

Despite my loyalty to you and my desperate need for funds...

GRATIANO

You need not do the deed yourself. You owe gambling debts
to villains with brutes in their employ who do not hesitate to
commit such crimes for a reasonable sum.

GRATIANO offers LODOVICO a purse full of
money which he does not take.

GRATIANO (Continued)

This purse contains enough to hire two such ruffians.

LODOVICO

But, an innocent...

GRATIANO

Clergymen and scholars insist these Moorish creatures are not human. If they were, would the church allow them to be sold as slaves?

GRATIANO offers the purse again. LODOVICO reluctantly accepts it. As he speaks, GRATIANO gets the blanket, offers it to LODOVICO.

GRATIANO (Continued)

Take this blanket with Brabantio's crest. Tell Bianca it's a present from Brabantio to his grandson. Give her urgent reason to wrap Antonio in the blanket so the brutes will know which baby to remove. Have the men disguise themselves as Moors. The purse provide sufficient funds to purchase robes, turbans, and dye that stains the skin. If someone witnesses the deed, two Moors were seen kidnapping the child.

LODOVICO

I am familiar with the Moors' peculiar dress and manner. I'll disguise myself as a Moor...

GRATIANO

You must not assume the risk.

LODOVICO

I can imitate a Moor to perfection.

GRATIANO

No, Lodovico.

LODOVICO

I can be a paragon of a Moor!

GRATIANO
(Physically abuses LODOVICO.)
Let the hirelings do the deed.

LODOVICO

As you say.

As GRATIANO speaks, HASSAN and
TOWNSPEOPLE enter with AFRICAN N.
Light intensifies on cradle.

GRATIANO

I'll take the ebony visitors to the convent. Their nearness to th
loathsome deed will paint them black as pitch. Have the
hirelings take the child to San Marco near the Grand Canal and
leave the corpse where it may easily be found in light of day.
We cannot have one dram of doubt about the dusky infant's
death.

As GRATIANO and LODOVICO exit,
CROSSFADE to...

SCENE SEVEN

TOWNSPEOPLE confront HASSAN.

TOWNSPEOPLE
An ocean of perfume cannot cover up their odious depravity.
What will you do to stop them?

HASSAN
Stop who? Stop what?

TOWNSPEOPLE
You cannot allow the murder an innocent child.

HASSAN
We are here to tell the story. We do not get to change it.

TOWNSPEOPLE
No contrivance of corruption can justify the murder of a child.

HASSAN
Only time reveals the harvest.

TOWNSPEOPLE
That is unacceptable.

HASSAN
You said you would be patient while I tell the story.

TOWNSPEOPLE
Our patience grows weary. We need assurance...

HASSAN
If you wait for tomorrow, tomorrow comes. If you don't wait
for tomorrow, tomorrow comes.

LIGHTS OUT ON SCENE, THEN UP on...

SCENE EIGHT

Outside the wrong convent, early afternoon.

SOMAIA and ELISSA enter.

SOMAIA
These convents are everywhere in Venice.

ELISSA
We must have tried them all by now.

SOMAIA
Surely this one is the last.

ELISSA
I'm too exhausted to visit another one.

SOMAIA
I promise this will be the last one we visit... if my child is here.
Hellooo! May we enter?

ELISSA
This dampness and chill causes me considerable distress.

SOMAIA
How can Venice contain so many orphans? Gratiano's words
led me to think we would only need to find one convent.

ELISSA
Who keeps reminding me that Gratiano cannot be trusted?
These children must have aunts and uncles who would gladly
care for them. Hellooooo!

SOMAIA

All the aunts and uncles and cousins in Venice seem to have
deserted their children. Perhaps Venetians do not feel as much
responsibility for their children as we do.

ELISSA

People everywhere cherish their children. Venetians cannot
differ from the rest of us that much. And yet, the nuns appear
to furnish the only family these children have.
          (ELISSA calls out with some urgency.)
Hellooooo! Perhaps the cries of the babies drown our
presence.
          (ELISSA to calls out with greater urgency.)
Helloooooooooo!

SOMAIA

What if these clouds forewarn us of Venetian animosity?

ELISSA

Venetian animosity cannot modify our course of action.

VOICE

We are not available.

ELISSA

We want to speak to the person who is responsible for the
children.

VOICE

Come back some other time. We are at prayer.

SOMAIA

We are looking for my brother's child.

VOICE

We have no children of your kind.

SOMAIA

May we come inside? You may have...

VOICE

You are not welcome here! Be off!

SOMAIA
(Continues to yell to VOICE inside.)
For women who spend most of their time in prayer, your
charity seems in very short supply!

VOICE

We owe you no consideration.

SOMAIA
(Yells to the VOICE inside.)
If I could find a way to gain entrance, I would rescue every
child from this den of iniquity.

VOICE

Be off, I say!

ELISSA
(Yells to the VOICE inside.)
I have never seen such rudeness from a woman who professes
piety!
(To Somaia as she walks away.)
Let us not tarry a moment longer.
(Returns. Yells To the VOICE inside.)
Have you ever heard of hospitality?

SOMAIA

We must learn to expect the worst from these Venetians.

ELISSA and SOMAIA exit, **CROSSFADE to...**

SCENE NINE

Outside the convent, early afternoon.

HASSAN and BIANCA are present, but in different areas.

HASSAN
(Speaks to the audience as GRIOT.)
Unfortunately, Elissa and Somaia's quest takes them farther and farther away from their goal. Meanwhile, at the convent where Tarik's baby resides, Bianca impatiently awaits Lodovico's return-- or, more precisely, she impatiently awaits his money.

HASSAN exits as LODOVICO enters. As the dialogue continues, LODOVICO takes out the purse, gives BIANCA some money, puts most of the money back in the purse. She puts the money down her bosom, gestures for more. He reluctantly gives her more. She puts it down her bosom.

LODOVICO
I have an urgent mission that requires your collaboration.

BIANCA
Why not collaborate at my apartment?

LODOVICO
Faithful execution fosters our prosperity.

BIANCA
I am preparing a feast far more delicious than any innkeeper provides. Would you like to sample the delicacies that await your pleasure this evening?

LODOVICO
A morsel... No Bianca... I shall not surrender to...

BIANCA
A tantalizing entree will gratify your hunger... then, a
delectable dessert.

LODOVICO
My mouth waters in anticipation... but my reputation will be
tarnished if a holy sister finds us...

BIANCA
The only sister who might find us here is Sister Anna, and if
she discovered us in some mischief, by the time she got inside
and found someone to tell, she would not remember what she
saw, and so, your precious reputation would remain intact.

LODOVICO
Gratiano, that is, Brabantio sends this blanket with his crest.

Gives blanket to Bianca.

LODOVICO (Continued)
When the Moors first behold the child, he must be wrapped in
this blanket. The blanket is to warn the Moors Brabantio
intends to claim custody of the infant.

BIANCA
Such a lovely piece of cloth.

LODOVICO
Can you arrange with the holy sisters to carry out Brabantio's
request?

BIANCA
I have never seen such fancy needlework.

LODOVICO
This matter is of great concern to Gra... Brabantio.

BIANCA
Does he have this done in Venice?

LODOVICO
Bianca, do you hear me? The child must be wrapped in this
blanket tonight.

BIANCA
He must have found a seamstress in the provinces.

LODOVICO
You have not been listening to me.

BIANCA
Earlier you said the Moors must get the child and go. Now,
you want the child wrapped in this blanket so the Moors will
know Brabantio seeks custody of the child. You seem to be
striving for opposite results, but I will do as you say.

LODOVICO
Thank you for this favor.

BIANCA
More delectable favors than this await you at my lodgings.

LODOVICO
As much as I crave your... banquet... I must attend to urgent
business now. Postponement of our affection will benefit us
both. As soon as I am finished, I'll rush to your apartment.
(MORE)

        He embraces Bianca, starts out, returns, embraces
        her more vigorously.

LODOVICO (Continued)
I cannot wait until this evening. Attend to the blanket as quickly as possible and meet me at your lodgings right away.

BIANCA and LODOVICO each exit hastily in different directions as HASSAN enters.

HASSAN
(Speaks to the audience as GRIOT.)
Now that Bianca has most of the money Gratiano gave to Lodovico, how can Lodovico accomplish Gratiano's plan?

FADE TO BLACK -- END OF ACT ONE

ACT TWO

SCENE TEN

PROLOGUE, ACT TWO

Drumming begins. HASSAN enters, followed by
TOWNSPEOPLE.

HASSAN
(Speaks to the audience as GRIOT.)
Now, that we have had a chance to refresh ourselves, our story
will continue. Just before we left, I posed a question: How can
Lodovico accomplish Gratiano's plan? Bianca has most of the
money Gratiano gave Lodovico. So, how can Lodovico
possibly...
(Sees TOWNSPEOPLE, speaks to them.)
Why are you here?

TOWNSPEOPLE
You must persuade Gratiano to abandon his plan.

HASSAN
Our intermission has not refreshed your patience. Remember,
"Impatient feet may walk into a snake pit."

TOWNSPEOPLE
The murder of a baby is unthinkable.

HASSAN
Sometimes the truth reveals unthinkable things.

TOWNSPEOPLE
We demand assurance that Gratiano's treachery will not be
allowed to...

HASSAN
(Starts to interrupt after "assurance" and persists.)
My duty requires me to speak the truth. I will speak the truth
and you cannot persuade me to do otherwise. Settle
yourselves, and I will continue the story. Remember your
promise to help me illustrate the story for our guests.

TOWNSPEOPLE exit.

HASSAN (Continued)
(Speaks to the audience as GRIOT.)
Time has passed and we have seen the fruits of Somaia's
impatience. I knew her longing to see the baby would conquer
her good judgment. So, I sent along a few additional men to
observe them from a distance and make certain they
encountered no danger. Although I must admit I was a bit
surprised by Elissa. Or I should say I was surprised Somaia
persuaded Elissa to abandon an opportunity to go shopping.

CROSSFADE to...

SCENE ELEVEN

The inn, quarters of HASSAN's party, later that day.

ELISSA, and SOMAIA enter with a tray containing a pot of tea, dried fruit, cheese, etc. ELISSA eats; SOMAIA does not.

ELISSA
I am exhausted... But, we cannot allow these Venetians to dishearten us.

SOMAIA
What are we going to tell Hassan when he asks about our purchases at the market?

ELISSA
An unpleasant truth is better than a pleasant lie.

SOMAIA
Hassan will find our impatience difficult to swallow. If you tell him where we went...

ELISSA
Even Hassan can swallow impatience when it is first dipped in honey.

HASSAN rushes in.

HASSAN
Did Gratiano find me absent?

ELISSA
The clock struck three some time ago but Gratiano has not arrived.

HASSAN
These Venetian bureaucrats require a detailed written
description of the simplest transaction.

SOMAIA
Before we finally see the child we made this voyage to fetch,
he'll be an old man with a long white beard.

HASSAN
*(ELISSA joins in. They say the same phrase, nearly in
   unison.)*
No matter how long the night, the day is sure to come.
   (To ELISSA.)
How did your bargaining work out?

ELISSA
Even their market women are devoid of hospitality. I will not
purchase a garment from a market woman who does not speak
to me.

SOMAIA
My joy diminishes each moment my son remains in this
dreadful place.

HASSAN
The character of these Venetians is revealed by their treatment
of the Jews.

SOMAIA
But the Jews are their countrymen, are they not?

HASSAN
They seem to hate the Jews even though the Jews are
Venetian. The Jews are required to live apart from the
Christians in an isolated section of the city they call the ghetto.
Massive iron gates confine the Jews to this ghetto after dark.
The homes that border the area are not permitted windows or
(MORE)

HASSAN (Continued)

doors that face outside. And, when they leave their special enclave, they must wear a particular kind of hat that identifies them as Jewish.

SOMAIA

(Jokingly.)

They can identify us without a special hat.

HASSAN

We must be mindful of the way Venetians treat the Jews. They crave riches more than they respect human life.

SOMAIA

These people must have driven Tarik to despair. They celebrated his valor, lavished him with prominence and wealth; but they had no use for him beyond his military service. They must have seen his marriage as just another prize.

ELISSA

Tarik must have trusted her and depended on her knowledge of Venetian customs. I pray she was the loyal loving wife he deserved.

SOMAIA

She did not forewarn him of the hatred and abuse they suffered.

ELISSA

Perhaps she failed to recognize the magnitude of evil in her kinsmen.

SOMAIA

Her kinsman Gratiano wears wickedness upon his head as though it were a crown.

HASSAN

But we must risk his treachery to gain his help.

SOMAIA

Somehow, he intends to use us to gratify his lust for riches.

HASSAN

Venetians believe our wits are weakened by the sun. Do not disabuse them of this notion.

SOMAIA

We must command their respect.

HASSAN

Truth does not inspire transformation of their opinions, but their disdain gives us an advantage. This morning, I have sold nearly all of Tarik's estate. I expect to sell the rest and set sail for home while Gratiano and his kin are discussing how ignorant we are. Let them learn to respect us after we are gone.

SOMAIA

I've heard it said Venetians are slaves to their clocks. Perhaps Gratiano awaits us at another place.

HASSAN

We must depart once our purpose here is done. While I complete my mission, you and Somaia go to the convent and settle the arrangements for the baby.

SOMAIA

How can we find the convent without Gratiano's help? We tried to find...

ELISSA
(Interrupts SOMAIA.)
Do not prolong this dinner with Gratiano by telling stories of
your travels and adventures.

HASSAN
I wish I could avoid this meal.

ELISSA
You take such delight in telling your stories, and Gratiano has
not heard them before.

HASSAN
These unbelievers do not wash before they eat.

SOMAIA
Water is everywhere in Venice. Why do they?...

HASSAN
They believe washing is ungodly.

ELISSA
Where are their baths?

HASSAN
The most pridefully devout among them wallow in their
filthiness. I have heard of a nun who gained acclaim by not
washing any part of her body for sixty years, except the tips of
her fingers when she entered the church.

ELISSA
I do not believe your stories. But, let their food remain
untouched.

HASSAN
I cannot abide the smell or taste of it. They use no spices to
enhance the flavor, nor do they thoroughly cook their meat, and
(MORE)

HASSAN (Continued)

I'm never confident a dish they serve contains no swine. Their
conduct at the table is so boorish that I cannot speak of the
details. The most despicable behavior I have seen among them
occurs after they consume too much of their intoxicating wine.

ELISSA

(To HASSAN as she eats.)
Have some cheese and fruit so hunger offers no excuse to eat
their food.

HASSAN

When a woman wishes food, she says, "prepare something for
the children."

SOMAIA

My father is impatient to speak the baby's name.

HASSAN

You have inherited his impatience.

ELISSA

This weather provokes my joints to ache. Hopefully this tea
will offer some relief.
(Offers tea to SOMAIA.)
Somaia, you need to have some...

SOMAIA

When I see my son and know he's well and under our
protection, my warmth for him will burn away this gloom.

HASSAN

Somaia, your patience has been commendable. I'll arrange for
transportation and a guide.

HASSAN starts to exit; goes "outside" their
private area.

ELISSA

Do not forget the quilt.

SOMAIA instantly produces the quilt.

SOMAIA

How could I forget? I'll wrap the baby in it at our first opportunity.

ELISSA

Soon he'll touch the quilt, and feel its warmth, and know his spirit connects to ours and to his ancestors.

GRATIANO enters, but "Outside" the Moors' private area.

GRATIANO

Good afternoon, Signior Hassan. Please forgive my tardiness.

HASSAN

Signior Gratiano! I postponed some other business to meet you here at three o'clock, but you did not arrive at the appointed hour. Now, I must attend to that business and so I will not be able to go with you and the ladies to the convent. Some of my men will accompany them to assure their safety.

ELISSA and SOMAIA go "outside."

GRATIANO

Ladies.

SOMAIA
(Does not open the quilt.)
The women of our family made a quilt.

ELISSA

We'll wrap the baby in it this evening.

GRATIANO

Uhhh, no! I must ask you not to take the blanket. The Reverend Mother does not permit the babies to receive gifts.

ELISSA

The quilt holds great significance for us and for the child.

GRATIANO

She wishes equal deference for every child in her care.

HASSAN

Leave the quilt with me. I'll bring it to the convent when I come.

GRATIANO

Yes, it is much better if we leave it here. My gondola awaits.

GRATIANO leads ELISSA and SOMAIA out.

HASSAN
(Speaks to the audience as GRIOT.)
I rejected the temptation to ask Elissa and Somaia if they enjoyed their tour of nearly every convent in Venice. They were in no mood for teasing and I had work to do. So, I went about my errands with as much dispatch as possible. Several hours passed before I completed my mission and returned to meet Gratiano at the Inn.

HASSAN exits. **CROSSFADE to...**

SCENE TWELVE

Outside the Inn, early evening.

The place reeks of stale beer, rowdy men and women seeking compensation for sexual favors. GRATIANO waits, fends off women's advances, cuts an apple with a weapon-sized knife and eats as HASSAN rushes in.

HASSAN
I hope I have not kept you waiting.

GRATIANO
I am sorry you were not here to enjoy the meal. The chef prepared an exquisite roast of beef served with a hearty red wine. Rare beef must be consumed while hot or the flavor is lost.

Cuts a piece of apple. Offers it to HASSAN.

HASSAN
(Declines the apple.)
I am delighted you enjoyed your food.

GRATIANO
My nephew tells me your business brings you to Venice frequently.

HASSAN
I bring leather goods to your finest shops.

GRATIANO
Are these products of your own making?

HASSAN

I still make some pieces, but I'm fully occupied traveling and selling merchandise.

GRATIANO

They say the finest leather products come from Morocco.
(Continues to cut the apple and eat.)

HASSAN

The goods I bring to Venice now are made by artisans I have trained. In my youth, I traveled to the kingdom of Ghana with a caravan of salt merchants. At our destination, the people purchased salt, of which they have none, with gold, which they have in abundant supply. Their most spectacular gold pieces are kept at their king's compound. One of their gold nuggets weighs as much as a three-year-old boy and is used by the king to tether his horse. Although gold nuggets were large and plentiful, the people would not part with them, nor would they reveal their source. But I left with something far more valuable than gold.

GRATIANO

What could they possibly have that is more valuable than gold?

HASSAN

Knowledge, Signior Gratiano, knowledge. During my travels with the salt merchants, I became fascinated by the fine quality of their leather goods, and eventually, my curiosity prevailed above my modesty and I developed an acquaintance with some leather artisans. They accepted me as a member of their family and taught me how to prepare fine leathers from the hides of goats, and to craft it into products.

GRATIANO

Is Venice the only place you sell your products?

HASSAN

We place merchandise in Tunis, Algiers, Rome, and Naples.
We no longer call at western European ports and even as we
sail the Mediterranean, we have reduced our cargoes to make
room for warriors to defend us from predators who capture
Africans and sell them into slavery. The slavers are legendary
for their ruthlessness. A man who attempts escape has his
fingers cut off or his eyes wrenched from the sockets. A
woman who refuses to submit to them has her nose severed
from her face.

GRATIANO

Christian men would never commit such cruelty.
        (Cuts himself another slice of the apple, eats it.)

HASSAN

The men who accumulate vast wealth from the slave trade do
not care to know about the brutish acts committed by the men
in their employ.

GRATIANO

No Venetian flag flies above a ship that carries human cargo,
nor do we harbor animosity for the Moors. Your nephew came
to Venice in bondage, yet he was made a full Venetian citizen.

HASSAN

I understand the slavers often find capital in Venice.

GRATIANO

Perhaps the Jews lend money to the slavers. Venice takes pride
in its pristine reputation. But the Jews debase our good name
and jeopardize our commerce while profiting from the parasitic
practice of usury.

HASSAN

How can a Jew lend money to a Christian unless the Christian
seeks to borrow money?

GRATIANO

Of course, but the Jews...

HASSAN

Your Proverbs proclaim the borrower is servant to the lender, do they not? Why do you blame the Jews?...

> FRANCESCO enters. He has had too much to drink, but he is not "falling down" drunk. He listens unobtrusively. GRATIANO hands a document to HASSAN which HASSAN reads carefully.

GRATIANO

This routine document frees you from the inconvenience of responding to solicitations against Othello's estate. I fear you shall be required to make a time-consuming trip to Venice over some minor entanglement that I could easily resolve on your behalf.

> FRANCESCO crosses to GRATIANO as HASSAN speaks.

HASSAN

I cannot find words to praise your willingness to sacrifice your time so I might avoid a minor inconvenience.

GRATIANO

Francesco, my son.

FRANCESCO

How could I be your son when I am certain you are not my father?

GRATIANO

Do not ridicule me before this visitor.

FRANCESCO

Now, I recognize you sir! You are Gratiano, brother to
Senator Brabantio. Your legendary virtue is renowned
throughout Venice.

GRATIANO

Do not revile me Francesco. Give honest assurance that I am...

FRANCESCO

I am nothing if not honest; and, honestly, I am not your son.
You are a wealthy nobleman, is that not so?   And so, if I were
your son, I would be a wealthy nobleman. Honored visitor, am
I a wealthy nobleman?

GRATIANO

You are not beyond my retribution.

FRANCESCO

You are a man of spotless white reputation while my father is a
hypocrite, a thief, an adulterer, and a wife beater. A man of
your grandiloquence would not beat his wife! But my father is
a feculent scoundrel who brutally beats my mother. I would
expose my father, but my mother values honor more than
justice.

GRATIANO

Do not force me to more punitive response.

FRANCESCO

Pervasive treachery saturates my father.
          (Picks up GRATIANO's knife.)

GRATIANO

You need not fear my treachery.

FRANCESCO

I fear my treachery. My father's fiendish blood flows through my veins. I might slink into my father's house while he sleeps and quietly, without waking my mother,
    (Threatens GRATIANO with knife.)
Slit his throat.

BIANCA enters.

BIANCA

Signior Gratiano, I assure you urgent cause inspires my presence. I know you do not approve of my involvement with Lodovico...

FRANCESCO sulks into a dark corner.

GRATIANO

What do you want?

BIANCA

I wish to speak with Lodovico, sir.

GRATIANO

He is not here.

BIANCA

Not here?

GRATIANO

He, too, is on an urgent mission. In Lodovico's absence, might you confide in me?

HASSAN stops reading the documents.

BIANCA

Might we converse in a more confidential place?

GRATIANO

I will not be seen lurking in a secluded place with the likes of you. Disclose your purpose.

BIANCA

I bring unfortunate information from the convent that is home to the child, Antonio. I grew up at the same convent. Now, I go there to help with the children...

GRATIANO

What unfortunate information?

BIANCA

Antonio has been kidnapped.

> HASSAN and GRATIANO speak at the same time.

HASSAN

Kidnapped?

GRATIANO

If you lie...

BIANCA

I speak the truth, sir.

GRATIANO
(To HASSAN.)
My attendant will conduct you to the convent. I'll join you later. But first, I'll organize a search.
(To BIANCA.)
You need concern yourself no longer.
(MORE)

> HASSAN has gathered the papers. He exits.
> BIANCA exits in a different direction.

GRATIANO (Continued)
(To the audience.)
A dozen patrons of this inn await my invitation to commit
whatever mayhem serves my purposes.
(To the MOB.)
My fellow Venetian citizens, please. Please hear me out. My
fellow Venetians, please allow me to interrupt your merriment.

> GRATIANO addresses the people at the inn who
> become the MOB. Drumming begins softly.
> GRATIANO pauses only when the MOB's noise
> forces him to. Throughout, MOB lines come from
> different individuals **not** in unison, and overlap.
> Each word need **not** be heard distinctly.

MOB
Sh-h-h-h, Listen to Signior Gratiano...What does he want with
us?...Pay no attention to him. ...Listen.

GRATIANO
Honor my distress with your attention.

MOB
Quiet!...Take heed....Listen!

GRATIANO
The grandson of Senator Brabantio has been kidnapped.

MOB
Kidnapped?...Who could do such a thing?...Why?...Who?...Are
you certain?...A baby?

GRATIANO
A man of Christian temperament could not commit this
fiendish act.

MOB

Vengeance! ...Prison is too good for them. We must avenge
this ungodly deed.

GRATIANO

Reason compels me to consider the Moors.

MOB

No! The Jews!...Godless heathens! None of them belong in
Venice!

GRATIANO

These Moors are even more diabolical than the Jews. Embers
of iniquity smolder beneath their eyes.

> Noise from the mob builds. Drumming, cymbals
> intensify the growing feeling of a mob.

MOB

Find the Moors!...It must be the Moors. ...The Moors are
beasts. ...Animals! ...Kill the savages!

GRATIANO

Look to your daughters.

MOB

They cannot be trusted! ...Protect our children! ...Save us!
...Get weapons!

GRATIANO

One rapacious Moor killed my brother's only daughter. Look
to your wives!

MOB

Protect us! ...What do you mean? ...Savages!

GRATIANO

These black and burly creatures have used witchcraft and magic to climb between Venetian sheets and make the beast with two backs.

MOB

Kill them! Animals! ...Run them out. ...They have no rights in Venice. ...Witchcraft! ...Devils!

GRATIANO

These alien creatures do not deserve consideration at our Venetian bar of justice.

MOB

Kill the Moors! ...They deserve to die! ...Make them suffer. ...Death to the Moors! ...The Moors must die! ...Retribution!

GRATIANO

The first to find the heinous Moors is obliged to run them through.

MOB

Yes! ...Run them through! ...Kill the Moors!

GRATIANO

Do you wish to see fair Venice fall victim to these Moors?

MOB

(Together.)
No-o-o-o-o!

GRATIANO

Get weapons and follow me to San Marco near the Grand Canal.

GRATIANO exits; FRANCESCO follows. The
MOB nearly tramples GRATIANO in their haste
to go after the Moors.

MOB

After them! ...San Marco! ...Get weapons! ...Death to the
Moors! ...Revenge! ...Murders!
     (All together.)
Death to the Moors!

FADE TO BLACK. Lights up on...

SCENE THIRTEEN

San Marco, near the Grand Canal, evening.

The MOB lines should seem random and overlap. The MOB's feeling approaches chaos intensified by drums. Human forms are not clearly visible. Amid the MOB's outbursts, we hear a baby cry. FRANCESCO lurks unobserved [except by the audience] throughout.

MOB

Catch the heathens! Stop the villains! You'll see Venetian justice! String up the black thieves! We are not safe with Moors among us!
     (More!)
Stop thief! Kill the blackguards! Protect our children! We'll have none of your bloody mischief here! Protect us from these animals!
     (More!)
Don't let them get away! Give the sooty villains their due! Down with the dastards! Spill their heathen blood. Black rogues!
     (More!)
Don't let the heathens get away! Protect our honor! Save our women and children from these animals! Black heathen! You have no place to hide in Venice!
     (More!)
Hold him while I run him through! Die, savages! Destroy the Moorish dogs! Punish the villains! What have they done?

          LODOVICO enters disguised as a Moor, running
          from the MOB. He does not have the baby.

LODOVICO

GRATIANOOOO!!! Where are you? Save me! In heaven's name, tell these fools who I am! Stop! This is a mistake!
          (MORE)

One of the MOB stabs LODOVICO in the back.

LODOVICO (Continued)
GRATIANOOOOOO!

MOB
No more of their black villainy! A bloody death is all you
deserve, you scum! Their blood for ours! Death and
damnation to all the Moorish jackals. Rout them out!
(More!)
Keep Venice pure and safe from mongrels and Moors! Give
the Moorish devils their due! Make certain the Moors are
dead. The beasts may only be pretending.
(More!)
Kill the Moorish devils! Run them through again! Let their
heathen blood flow. Kill the savages! Are you sure they're
dead?

Silence. The baby is no longer crying.

MOB (Continued)
The baby is dead! The Moors have killed a baby. The baby is
dead? Who would kill a baby? Oh, no!
(More!)
The Moors have killed a baby. How could they? The Moorish
dogs deserve to die! Kill the savages! Death and damnation
to your heathen clan!

GRATIANO enters, lantern in hand, assumes both
corpses are hired assassins, goes to LODOVICO.

GRATIANO
Justice has been served, my friends and comrades! You'll be
rewarded for dispensing retribution to these Moorish monsters
who kidnapped and killed an innocent baby. All Venetians
will rest easier tonight. Take away the poor infant and the
heartless brutes who murdered him.
(MORE)

> Baby and assassin are carried off. The figure still lurks where the audience sees him but cannot distinguish his identity. GRATIANO turns the body over and discovers it's LODOVICO.

                    GRATIANO (Continued)
Noooo! Leave this one here awhile.
> *(Addresses the corpse of LODOVICO after the others are gone.)*

My poor dear Lodovico, why did you take on this bloody job yourself? You were supposed to hire two assassins. What recklessness persuaded you to wear this lethal masquerade?
> *(Notices FRANCESCO hiding in the shadows.)*

Who's there? Francesco, my son. Is that you? How long have you been there? What do you make of these repulsive deeds?
> *(FRANCESCO does not reply.)*

The baby Moor is dead.
> *(Still no response.)*

Whatever has estranged us must be put aside. I beseech you to be loyal to your family. The people who pursued the kidnappers thought they were Moors. We must not say otherwise for fear we will incriminate Brabantio. I fear my brother has come unhinged. He swore he would rather see Antonio dead than given to the Moors. Although I fear this deadly scheme may be my brother's fabrication, we cannot be certain.
> *(Still no response.)*

Will you go and tell the Reverend Mother of the infant's death? Please, my son. I need to stay with Lodovico and see that proper arrangements are made.

> The shadowy figure exits without speaking.
> **CROSSFADE to...**

SCENE FOURTEEN

HASSAN is alone in another place.

HASSAN
(To the audience as GRIOT.)
Even Gratiano tells the truth occasionally. It's true! Earlier, he
promised to show Elissa and Somaia to the convent they could
not find on their own. And sure enough, they arrived as
quickly as he promised. The Reverend Mother greeted Elissa
and Somaia, explained she had matters which demanded her
attention and abruptly disappeared. The nuns would not allow
my family to see the child or discuss their plan to raise the
child in Africa. Just as Somaia was about to explode from this
blatant breech of hospitality, pandemonium swept through the
convent. They discovered one of the babies was missing.
Someone screamed...

VOICE
Little Antonio has been kidnapped!

HASSAN
Elissa and Somaia sought more information, but the sisters
only smiled and offered food and tea. Somaia was about to
search for the baby on her own, when suddenly, the Reverend
Mother favored the visitors with her attention.

CROSSFADE to...

SCENE FIFTEEN

The Chapter House of the Convent, later that evening.

ELISSA, and SOMAIA are present. REVEREND MOTHER enters. She carries a bible which she places nearby. Initially, she does not deem to focus full attention on ELISSA and SOMAIA.

SOMAIA

The baby must depart with us as soon as he is found.

REVEREND MOTHER

We have not confirmed the missing infant is your nephew.

SOMAIA

And we have not confirmed the baby is actually missing.

REVEREND MOTHER

Are you accusing me...?

ELISSA
(Tries to be conciliatory.)
Why do these uncertainties arise after our arrival?

REVEREND MOTHER

I vowed to celebrate the glory of God. Instead, I'm chasing villains.

ELISSA

This must be the work of slave traders!

REVEREND MOTHER

We have no slave traders here.

ELISSA

My husband visits Venice frequently, and he has observed purchasers and sellers of human flesh with disgusting regularity.

SOMAIA

Venetians piously profess opposition to capturing and selling human souls, yet they harvest riches of incredible magnitude from investments they make in the corrupt commerce.

ELISSA

Are you so sheltered here you know nothing of these repugnant practices?

REVEREND MOTHER

Security and quietude prevailed within this sanctuary. Suddenly you people appear and this holy place is drenched in malice.

SOMAIA

The baby cannot be rescued by unsubstantiated charges. Nor will kidnappers be captured by false accusations.

ELISSA

We are strangers in your city and strangers even more to your customs and traditions. We mean no disrespect, but we intend to secure our rightful heir and take him home.

REVEREND MOTHER

The child remains under my protection until I choose a suitable family. If none is found, he shall remain with us.

SOMAIA

We are this baby's family. You have no right...

ELISSA

You seem preoccupied with making decisions that are not
yours to make. Somaia is the baby's rightful guardian.

SOMAIA

(To ELISSA.)
This woman speaks to us as a lion speaks to a jackal.
(To the REVEREND MOTHER.)
Your indifference cuts as sharp and cold as a sword. You seem
to take great pride in purging compassion from your
considerations. You say you only value rational things.

REVEREND MOTHER

Our decisions are not based on sentiment.

SOMAIA

It seems that all things rational have been written in your books
containing rules. Every issue we raise invites the recitation of
a rule.

REVEREND MOTHER

We are governed by the Universal...

SOMAIA

...rules, which permit you to reach conclusions without the use
of either mind or heart.

REVEREND MOTHER

We are bound by the laws of our lord and savior as interpreted
by the church.

SOMAIA

God would not create laws that deprive a mother of a child and
a child of a mother.

REVEREND MOTHER
I am sincerely moved by your eloquent aspiration. But I derive
my authority from the church. And the church decrees all
souls belong to the church.

ELISSA
When we arrived, you thanked Signior Gratiano for the gifts he
has provided for the child; yet, Signior Gratiano admonished
us not to bring a gift. He told us you do not allow gifts.

REVEREND MOTHER
I have never denied a gift to any of our children.

ELISSA
What would Signior Gratiano gain by depriving a baby of a
quilt?

HASSAN enters.

REVEREND MOTHER
I assure you I do not know.

SOMAIA
(Quietly.)
Signior Gratiano's lies obscure your view like sand in a desert
storm.

ELISSA
Oh Hassan, have you heard what happened?

HASSAN
We were told the child was kidnapped. Gratiano is organizing
a search party.

SISTER ANNA runs in, speaks before HASSAN
finishes.

SISTER ANNA

Reverend Mother, little Antonio, has been found. He is sleeping exactly where I left him when I went to evening prayer.

All respond at once. Speeches overlap.

REVEREND MOTHER

O thank God!

ELISSA

Oh Hassan, they didn't take our baby.

SOMAIA

My baby is safe after all.

HASSAN

Praise be to Allah.

Overlapping response ends.

SISTER ANNA

There is a missing baby...

REVEREND MOTHER

But, you said...

SISTER ANNA

Sister Maria and I were on our way to the nursery. I had little Guiseppi in my arms. Reverend Mother, I know you tell me I hold the children too much. But little Guiseppi is so young and needs affection.

REVEREND MOTHER

Sister Anna, please...

SISTER ANNA

Forgive my diversion. This excitement distracts me more than... We encountered little Bianca as we were going into the nursery. I still call her little Bianca. I attended to her when she was a baby here.

REVEREND MOTHER

Sister Anna...

SISTER ANNA

And so, Bianca appeared to be in quite a hurry. She gave me a blanket and said it was a gift from Signior Brabantio to his grandson. The needlework is superb. Sister Maria said it must have come from Florence. Such fine craftsmanship...

REVEREND MOTHER

Please continue...

SISTER ANNA

Bianca gave me the blanket and rushed away. As I carried little Guiseppi, I must have covered him in the blanket. Then, another child began to cry--little Giancarlo, I believe it was. So I put Guiseppi down. By the time Giancarlo had quieted himself, Sister Bettina reminded me I was about to be late for evening prayer. So, I hurried off and completely forgot about the blanket. After evening prayer, Sister Maria noticed one of the babies was missing. Bianca inquired if the missing baby was wrapped in the blanket with Signior Brabantio's crest. Sister Maria said yes and Bianca screamed "Antonio has been kidnapped!" and rushed away. I had intended to wrap little Antonio in the blanket, but I became so distracted by...

REVEREND MOTHER

Sister Anna, please...

SISTER ANNA
There is no doubt little Antonio is exactly where I left him.
Although we never speak of his complexion, we see the
difference between Antonio and the other children.

SOMAIA
Brabantio is responsible for the kidnapping.

REVEREND MOTHER
You have no evidence...

SOMAIA
Brabantio sent his blanket to mark the baby.

HASSAN
The baby is not safe here. We must fetch him and depart at
once.

REVEREND MOTHER
Who is this man?

ELISSA
He is my husband. The child you call Antonio is his heir.

HASSAN
I am Hassan Ben Akbar.

REVEREND MOTHER
(To Elissa.)
Why do you avoid calling the child Antonio?

SOMAIA
His father's name was Tarik, and you called him Othello. We
would not suppose you would treat his son with more
consideration.

REVEREND MOTHER
We care for little Antonio as lovingly as anyone could expect.
I shall no longer concern myself with your feelings. And in
that spirit, I must inform you that you may not take the child.

SOMAIA
Your spirit has not changed since our arrival. First, you ignore
us. Then you tell us you have authority to keep a member of
our family confined to this convent as if he is a prisoner. You
cannot create a family by stealing other people's children. If
you wish to have children, why did you take a vow of chastity?

REVEREND MOTHER
The laws of the church grant me authority.

SOMAIA
Your authority cannot deny this baby has a family. We are his
family, and we are here to take him home.

HASSAN
(In contrast to SOMAIA's hostility.)
I am perplexed by your interpretation of the laws, but I respect
your devotion and admire the charity you provide these
innocents. How do you support your noble deeds?

REVEREND MOTHER
(Appreciates the gentler tone.)
We have ample grounds to produce most of our food. But
beyond providing sustenance and shelter, our assets are quite
meager.

HASSAN
I'm sure my kinsman whom you call Othello would wish to
leave a significant part of his estate as an expression of his
gratitude for the care you have provided for his son.

REVEREND MOTHER
We are most appreciative of all donations.

HASSAN
Our faith allows us to honor the principles others choose. We merely seek to practice our beliefs in peace.

REVEREND MOTHER
We pray for universal peace.

HASSAN
Is the man you call Othello father of the child you call Antonio?

REVEREND MOTHER
(Her tone is no longer hostile.)
Signior Hassan, you know I cannot speak to fatherhood. I was not present when the child was conceived.

HASSAN
(Continues his kinder gentler approach.)
Is Desdemona the mother of this child?

REVEREND MOTHER
I swore I would never reveal the mother's identity. But you may look upon the countenance of the infant. Further evidence may not be necessary.

HASSAN
My sacred covenant requires me to provide for the children God bestows and show them the ancient landmarks along the path of righteousness. I cannot allow this child to be raised apart from his kin so long as I draw breath and have shelter for myself. No human force can alter this covenant. Since Desdemona's father is family to this child as well, we will make every effort to resolve our goals in harmony with his intentions.

REVEREND MOTHER
Signior Brabantio has refused past invitations to share his
plans with us. But, I see no harm in asking him again.

HASSAN
Meanwhile, please allow us to see the child.

REVEREND MOTHER
Sister Anna, will you please fetch the child? The ladies may
accompany you if they wish.

All except HASSAN exit.

ELISSA
(To REVEREND MOTHER as they exit.)
Reverend Mother, since you do not prohibit gifts to the
children, do you not find it strange that Signior Gratiano would
not allow us to give the child a quilt?

CROSSFADE to...

SCENE SIXTEEN

HASSAN as GRIOT crosses to another place.

TOWNSPEOPLE enter wearing African masks.

HASSAN
The story does not require your presence at this time.

TOWNSPEOPLE
We are here to express concern over the way you are handling
this matter. We wish to appeal to your better judgment.

HASSAN
Are you asking me to fabricate?

TOWNSPEOPLE
You must allow Brabantio to keep the child!

HASSAN walks away in disgust and disbelief.

TOWNSPEOPLE (Continued)
Our voices must be heard. We speak for ourselves and for
generations to come. They call Tarik "Othello" and claim he
murdered his wife in a fit of savage jealousy. But there is no
evidence to support their claim. If Brabantio is allowed to
raise the child, Antonio's virtue will overturn this pernicious
fabrication. He will learn to imitate the manners of a Venetian
nobleman and the Venetians will come to see this Moorish
child as human. When they do, all of us will be human in their
eyes.

HASSAN
Do you recall what happened to Tarik? If the child remains in
Venice, he will become accustomed to their ways. Over time
he will feel compelled to serve their greed and treachery.

TOWNSPEOPLE

If the child remains in Venice, his virtue will show them we are not murderers and savages. Your goal only benefits your family's narrow personal concerns. You must consider what is best for all of us.

HASSAN

When the Venetians encounter one of us, they see Othello the beast. No amount of evidence will alter their perception. Venetians say Othello was noble and profound; and yet, they saw him as a savage.

TOWNSPEOPLE

Paradox, irony, contradiction.

HASSAN

We cannot win their favor by putting on their customs and beliefs as if we were putting on their garments. Since their view of us is not rooted in reason, we cannot expect reason to alter their view of us. And yet, you would have us abandon our child to these Venetians in some vain and worthless effort to disguise yourself as one of them! Is Venetian approval a reasonable price for your self-respect?

Gets no response. **CROSSFADE to...**

SCENE SEVENTEEN

The Chapter House of the Convent, about one hour later.

REVEREND MOTHER, BRABANTIO, SOMAIA, and ELISSA are present. HASSAN joins them.

REVEREND MOTHER
You sent a blanket with your crest this afternoon, did you not?

BRABANTIO
My crest?

REVEREND MOTHER
Apparently, the blanket was a signal for the kidnappers. Little Guiseppi was kidnapped because he was wrapped in the blanket with your crest.

BRABANTIO
My brother took such a blanket. But, I did not suspect it would be used to mark an innocent child.

REVEREND MOTHER
Then, you agree the villains came for Antonio, using the blanket as a sign of his identity.

BRABANTIO
I'm confident we can arrange for the child's safe return.

SOMAIA
(To REVEREND MOTHER.)
Only knowledge of the crime could foster such decisive confidence.

HASSAN
(To BRABANTIO)
Do you know about a mission Lodovico was required to carry
out this evening?

BRABANTIO
(Ignores HASSAN, speaks to the REVEREND MOTHER.)
What is the victim's name?

REVEREND MOTHER
Guiseppi.

BRABANTIO
If the villains demand payment for Guiseppi's safe return, I
will provide his ransom as if he were my own Antonio.

REVEREND MOTHER
Your own Antonio? Gratiano repeatedly informed me you
have no interest in Antonio.

BRABANTIO
I have spent these last few weeks in diligent pursuit of
authority to make Antonio my heir.

REVEREND MOTHER
I solicited your collaboration and you answered my courtesy
with insult. After you learned Antonio's coloration is more
swarthy like a Moor, you cursed your daughter for conceiving
a child with Othello, cursed the church for sanctioning her
marriage, and blasphemed this convent for keeping mother and
baby safe through childbirth. Do you deny your profane
words?

BRABANTIO
When my brother discovered your plan to offer custody of my
grandson to the Moors, I was overcome...

REVEREND MOTHER
I did not offer custody of Antonio to the Moors, nor did I ever plan to do so. But, we cannot ignore the relationship between the kidnapping and your blanket.

FRANCESCO enters.

FRANCESCO
Good evening Reverend Mother, Uncle Brabantio, one and all. I must use bitter words to convey bitter deeds. My cousin, Lodovico, has been murdered.

All respond at once.

BRABANTIO
That cannot be! You must be mistaken.

REVEREND MOTHER
May God bless Lodovico.

ELISSA
What a terrible misfortune!

HASSAN
May Allah give us peace.

FRANCESCO interrupts.

FRANCESCO
There is more sorrow. The infant who was taken from this convent has been murdered.

All respond at once.

BRABANTIO
My brother would not do such a thing.

REVEREND MOTHER
May God bless poor little Guiseppi.

SOMAIA
These people have no shame.

HASSAN
Where is Gratiano? He must be held accountable.

FRANCESCO continues.

FRANCESCO
My father's perverse tongue inflamed a band of rowdies to
charge into the night in search of justice. When I approached,
I found a dim tableau-- baby murdered-- two men appearing to
be Moors. The drunken mob attacked and quickly slew both
men.

HASSAN and SOMAIA respond at once.

HASSAN
My countrymen?

SOMAIA
Without a chance to offer explanation or defense!

FRANCESCO
The men pretended to be Moors. They stained their faces to a
Moorish hue and dressed in robes and turbans. And one of
them was Lodovico.

HASSAN
Gratiano said Lodovico was on a mission. What do you know
about his mission?

FRANCESCO

I knew nothing of this obscene collusion until after the deeds were done.

HASSAN

What do you know now?

FRANCESCO

I know my father directed Lodovico to hire two assassins, disguise them as Moors, kidnap the infant wrapped in Brabantio's blanket, and murder the infant.

BRABANTIO

Gratiano must pay for his diabolic deeds.

ELISSA

What punishment can atone for the murder of a child?

BRABANTIO

Our laws mandate his immediate execution.

REVEREND MOTHER

May his soul rest in peace.

BRABANTIO

Reverend Mother, I have wrongfully accused you. Please accept my most devout apology.

FRANCESCO

Do not condemn Signior Brabantio. Reliance on his brother was his only fault.

> HASSAN gives papers to BRABANTIO who takes them without acknowledging HASSAN and begins to read.

HASSAN

Gratiano requested me to sign these papers. I'm not sure if I am more perturbed by his brazen deceit or his contempt for my intelligence.

ELISSA takes SOMAIA aside, speaks to her confidentially as BRABANTIO reads the papers.

ELISSA

Surely this woman will not entrust a child to Brabantio.

SOMAIA

Does the title "Reverend Mother" make her different from the others?

ELISSA

I pray she is a pious woman who only wants to do what is best for the child.

SOMAIA

I would pray too, but my prayers only seem to rain down havoc. I cannot give birth to my own children, but I know I can be a good mother. Have the ancestors forsaken me? Does my suffering beget another generation of suffering?

ELISSA

Your suffering is over. The ancestors will protect you, Somaia.

SOMAIA

Does this curse extend to my brother's child as well? What is the price he must pay for surviving this terrible night? To live in Venice and learn to be someone he is not?

ELISSA

The ancestors did not save him from assassins only to force him to endure such a fate.

BRABANTIO
(Still ignores HASSAN, speaks to REVEREND MOTHER.)
This document seeks to transfer ownership of Othello's entire
estate to Gratiano. How could my brother conceive of such a
vile, despicable, avaricious...

HASSAN
Of course, there was no collusion on your part. Your only
fault was to trust your brother.

BRABANTIO
(Still ignores HASSAN, speaks to REVEREND MOTHER.)
Reverend Mother, I deserve your reprimand. But, I pray you
will release Antonio to my care.

REVEREND MOTHER
I intend to place Antonio with his rightful family. But what is
rightful remains muddled.

HASSAN
(Refuses to allow BRABANTIO to ignore him further.)
Have you considered the repercussions? If you declare
yourself the grandfather, your noble status among Venetians
will diminish as a burning building is reduced to ashes.

BRABANTIO
I pledge my time and resources to help Antonio overcome the
misfortune of his birth.

SOMAIA
His only misfortune is to be born in Venice.

FRANCESCO
I must atone for the sorrow of this occasion and repudiate my
father. I ask you, Uncle Brabantio for devotion and counsel.
In all things, please consider me your son.

BRABANTIO

Henceforth, I am your father.

REVEREND MOTHER
(To BRABANTIO.)
You have demonstrated fitness as a Christian father by raising Desdemona to maturity. In keeping with our laws, the child is yours.

SOMAIA

Brabantio's blanket marked the child for murder.

BRABANTIO

Antonio is my entitlement. Among your people, he would become cruel and savage like his father.

SOMAIA

If the child remains in Venice, he will become a Venetian-- greedy, selfish, and arrogant, with no regard for family or community.

HASSAN
(Seeks to quiet SOMAIA's angry name-calling tone.)
Your faith proclaims, "Treat all God's children as you would have others treat you." Yet, Christians brutalize women from my homeland without remorse or fear of violating Christian virtues, professing people of my hue are not human. If our women are human, they deserve your deference. If they are beasts, an act of fornication is as vile as it would be with any other beast.

REVEREND MOTHER

How dare you speak of such depravity in this holy place!

SOMAIA

Depravity is more abundant here than water.

BRABANTIO
My wealth and station shield Antonio.

HASSAN
(Continues to seek a quiet, rational tone.)
In Venice, no enormity of rank and riches can protect a child
of Moorish parentage. I cannot abandon this child in a place
where many people consider him less than a dog. We embrace
this child as one of us. If the child remains, can you assure me--
can you assure yourself-- that your fellow Christians will not
throw stones at him and call him heathen, uncivilized, and
savage? Can you assure us your people will not defile his
mother and call him mongrel for no reason other than his hue?

REVEREND MOTHER
Moors are not only safe but welcome here.

HASSAN
I believe you to be honest and sincere; but I have been to
Venice many times before wearing the skin I wear today.
When seen through my eyes, Venice is a different place than it
appears when seen through yours.

ELISSA
(To BRABANTIO.)
Does your Venetian nobility guarantee the child will not be
abducted and sold as a slave?

HASSAN
(To BRABANTIO.)
Think of the humiliation this child must endure if he remains
here. If you love him, do not force him to suffer so.

BRABANTIO
No matter how convincingly you argue, Antonio is my
grandson.

HASSAN

Each of us holds membership in the human race; yet, some
Christians boast of purity in a race that excludes the rest of us.
As long as humankind has moved about the earth, people of
one place have intermingled with people from another. Is the
child of Desdemona and Tarik impure because his parents
come from different places? I love this child no less because
his mother was Venetian. Do you love this child no less
because his father was a Moor?

(BRABANTIO does not ANSWER.)

Such rancor over a baby still in swaddling. A dimpled infant
may amuse your friends, but will they be amused when he's old
enough to notice their daughters? All your wealth and power
cannot disguise his color when he seeks affection from their
daughters. And what befalls the maiden who reveals an
earnest interest in this Moor? Will she be abused and
disavowed by her father as Desdemona was?

(BRABANTIO still does not answer.)

We are peaceful people and wish no harm to anyone. Still, I
have a sacred obligation to provide the child a home. I have
been fortunate to accumulate some wealth and influence among
my people as you have among yours. I could return to Venice
with several thousand men whose military skills and valor
nearly equal Tarik's.

BRABANTIO

You would resort to military conflict?

(HASSAN does not answer.)

Whoever provides for the child would surely wish to keep
Othello's fortune.

HASSAN

If the child returns with us, we will depart as soon as possible.
We trust you to hold the future of your grandson uppermost.
His properties will survive beyond my years and yours.

BRABANTIO

The governor urged me, for the well-being of the Venetian state, to give my only child in marriage to a man who had betrayed my confidence.

HASSAN

(Gently interrupts.)
Let us abandon the matters that divide us. We are united by our aspiration to provide the best for our heir.

BRABANTIO

The weight of your argument crushes my resolve. I agree we are connected by the child. Each of us enjoys an advantage over the other. You can provide family for the child, while my proximity to Othello's fortune renders me the rational choice to oversee its management.

HASSAN

I agree. You will oversee the management of all Tarik's properties remaining here in Venice after we have safely departed with the child.

BRABANTIO

Since the Reverend Mother has granted responsibility for Antonio to me, I profess authority to transfer guardianship to you. Reverend Mother, I ask you to present Antonio to his family so they may commence their voyage. Francesco is my legacy.

REVEREND MOTHER

Signior Brabantio, I concede your authority to delegate responsibility for Antonio. But, I rebuke you for failing to provide a Christian home for a child born into my care and protection.
(To ELISSA and SOMAIA.)
Please accompany me.

> HASSAN gives the quilt to SOMAIA.
> REVEREND MOTHER escorts ELISSA and
> SOMAIA to another area where SISTER ANNA
> enters with the baby, gives him to SOMAIA, and
> exits. ELISSA opens the quilt and covers the
> baby. REVEREND MOTHER moves to the
> background.

HASSAN

(To BRABANTIO.)

Regardless of our differences, the child unites us. We welcome
you into our home as family. Your grandson will be taught to
love you and respect you. We bid you peace.

> BRABANTIO does not reply. HASSAN goes to
> ELISSA and SOMAIA. BRABANTIO and
> FRANCESCO remain. Subsequently, neither
> group hears or sees the other.
>
> BRABANTIO is "alone" with FRANCESCO.

BRABANTIO

Francesco, my son, we must exploit this opportunity to seize
Othello's fortunes on my behalf. In time, you will inherit them
from me.

> BRABANTIO and FRANCISCO exit. HASSAN,
> ELISSA, SOMAIA, and REVEREND MOTHER
> remain.

ELISSA

(To HASSAN.)

You said you would make certain this baby inherits Tarik's
estate.

HASSAN

And so I have. Tarik's properties within the city have all been
sold and the proceeds from the sale are secure aboard our
vessel. Reverend Mother, I have transferred ownership of
Tarik's olive groves and vineyards to the convent. In my
opinion, they are more valuable if you keep the land and sell
the produce. But, the land is yours to sell if you choose.

REVEREND MOTHER

How can I thank you?

HASSAN

Remember your "little Antonio" in your prayers. I will make
certain he remembers you in his.

As SOMAIA and ELISSA depart with the baby,
CROSSFADE to...

SCENE EIGHTEEN

EPILOGUE -- HASSAN's village in Africa

HASSAN speaks as he walks out of the previous scene. Music begins.

HASSAN
(Speaks to the audience as GRIOT.)

Brabantio insisted I remain in Venice long enough to witness Gratiano's execution. Fortunately for us, Gratiano was captured that very evening and executed at sunrise the next day. Before the Bank of St. George opened and Brabantio discovered nothing remained of Tarik's estate for him to squander, we set sail for home with all of Tarik's fortunes.

SOMAIA and ELISSA join HASSAN. As TOWNSPEOPLE enter, they sing and dance to welcome SOMAIA, ELISSA, HASSAN and the BABY home. SOMAIA, ELISSA, and HASSAN take the BABY to his CRADLE and place him in it. The dancing and singing continues until... **THE LIGHTS FADE. THE END.**

Overcoming Double Consciousness:
Exploring *Fortunes of The Moor*
— Barbara J. Molette and Carlton W. Molette

Nearly a century ago, W. E. B. DuBois identified a phenomenon he called "double consciousness" which helps to illuminate the difficulty, maybe even the impossibility, for African Americans to achieve a culturally centered position. DuBois described double consciousness as, "the sense of always looking at one's self through the eyes of others, ... One ever feels his twoness--an American, a Negro, two souls, two thoughts, two unreconciled strivings...."[1]   Neither Afrocentric nor Eurocentric views represent "human nature" or a world view. Each is simply a "location" from which phenomena are viewed. We use the terms "place," "location" and "centered position" in the sense that Molefe Kete Asante uses these terms in his seminal work *The Afrocentric Idea*[2] and contends, "...the most rewarding results of any analysis of culture derive from a centered position, usually defined as the *place* from which all concepts, ideas, purposes, and vision radiate." Afrocentric and Eurocentric theatre differ in the place from which a play is conceived by its playwright(s) and observed by its audience.

In 1997, an opportunity to confront our own double-consciousness presented itself as an invitation to workshop our

---

[1] W.E.B.DuBois, *The Souls of Black Folk* (1903; rpt. New York: New American Library, l969), 45.

[2] *The Afrocentric Idea* was published in 1987, but a more succinct statement appears in Asante's essay, "Location Theory and African Aesthetics," published in *African Aesthetics: Keeper of the Traditions*, edited by Kariamu Welsh-Asante, p.4.

play *Fortunes of The Moor* with Abibigromma [the National Theatre Company of Ghana] and later present the play at the University of Ghana in Legon, Ghana's National Theatre in Accra, and Panafest '97 [Pan-African Historical Theatre Festival] in Cape Coast. The opportunity enabled us to discover the extent to which the pervasive impact of Eurocentricism had shaped early iterations of the script and shift the play's location while working in a more Afrocentric environment.

We derived our initial inspiration for the play from a three-sided debate among government officials, social workers and potential adoptive parents over whether or not White families should be allowed to adopt Black children. We were not surprised in the mid-nineteen-seventies that questions about Black families adopting White children and what is a "mixed-race" child and who should be allowed to adopt one seemed off limits to similar public consideration. Although we discussed the idea of a play about the "mixed race" son of Othello and Desdemona back then, we did not begin work on *Fortunes of The Moor* until 1993.

Following readings at the Frank Silvera Writers Workshop and the National Black Theatre Festival, the play premiered at the Frank Silvera Writers Workshop in New York with productions soon after at Western Michigan University and the Connecticut Repertory Theatre. The Ohio State University had already scheduled a production for 1998 when we were invited to develop a production at Abibigromma in the summer of 1997.

Before we began to think about the Ghanaian production of *Fortunes of The Moor*, we were already familiar with Molefi Asante's concept of location. But our familiarity with the concept was more theoretical than we recognized. Developing *Fortunes of The Moor* for Ghana demanded that we consider our location in more concrete practical behavioral terms. In the vernacular, we had to evolve from talking the talk to walking the walk. After decades of earnest endeavor to write from a more Afrocentric location, we were forced to admit the place from which we originally envisioned *Fortunes of The Moor* was more Eurocentric than we had realized or intended. As we began to think about creating the play in Ghana with an all-Ghanaian cast, we started to conceptually (unconsciously) relocate the play. Once we were actually in Ghana, we were surrounded by constant reminders that a Eurocentric view is not a world view. Our physical location stimulated our intellectual and spiritual relocation and enabled– even required– us to relocate the play to a more African place.

We summarize the play here as we initially conceived it in order to describe the changes we made in Ghana. As Shakespeare's *Othello* concludes, Desdemona and Othello are dead and Lodovico, Desdemona's cousin urges his uncle Gratiano to "seize upon the fortunes of the Moor." Later, Gratiano learns that Desdemona secretly gave birth to a boy who remains at the Venetian convent where Desdemona took refuge after her father, Brabantio, disowned her. Venetian law makes her baby heir to both Othello's and Brabantio's fortune. Gratiano's greed motivates him to send his nephew Lodovico to Africa to find Othello's family and convince them to claim the child. Gratiano is in the midst of a scheme to "borrow" Brabantio's money, without his knowledge, so he can invest in a slave ship. But once Brabantio discovers the child's existence, he declares his intent to make the child his heir. Gratiano thinks his racist references to the child's heritage will persuade Brabantio to abandon interest in the child. After Othello's family arrives to claim the child, Gratiano realizes Brabantio still wants the child. So Gratiano plots with Lodovico to have some thugs kidnap and murder the child. Lodovico bungles the job and Gratiano's web of murder and deceit unravels. Ultimately, both Brabantio and Othello's family each believe they have seized the best of Othello's legacy.

Since the advent of realism, a pervasive convention of Eurocentric theatre has been the illusion of eavesdropping. The location of the playwright's concept and the audience's view offers direct observation of events unfolding in a linear time narrative. Originally, *Fortunes of The Moor* was conceived in this Eurocentric convention which allowed the audience to look directly into Venice in 1565. The action moved in linear time.

The audience eavesdrops as Gratiano discusses the investment he plans to make in a slave ship and as he tries to get Brabantio to disavow his grandson with such innuendos as "What if the savage disposition of the father simmers in the son?" The play's representational style seemed to emerge from Gratiano's perspective and focus on his dilemma.

The Venetians in our play were Venetian and they were located in Venice. We thought a play set in Venice in the late 1500's using traditional Western theatre conventions and expressing an Afrocentric point of view about obvious issues implied but not addressed, in Shakespeare's *Othello* would generate interest among theatre programs that consider the production of Shakespeare's plays to be among their strengths– large predominately White universities and regional professional theatres. In addition, we thought such theatres would consider the mix of characters (eight Venetians and three Africans) good for their proclaimed diversity goals.

In anticipation of our work in Ghana, we began to revise the script for a company of Ghanaian actors whose appearance did not offer the "racial differences" earlier iterations of the script demanded. As we began to re-structure *Fortunes of The Moor* for a Ghanaian cast and audience, we began to discover the Eurocentricism inherent in some of our earlier assumptions. Conversations with Mohammed Ben Abdallah, Ph.D., former Minister of Culture and founder of Abibigromma, before and during our stay in Ghana enhanced this discovery process and generated a series of changes.

The pivotal change located the play's action in Africa. Africans tell the story narratively and portray the action dramatically. The story is told in Abibigoro– an African style that is presentational and interactive. In Abibigoro, the location of the playwright's concept can be inside the "room" of the story and the audience can be a part of the action. Changing the locale to Africa facilitated a change in the way we thought about costumes, scenery, and props from one of accurate observation of the artifacts of Venice in the 1500's to one that presumes the artifacts used in the play come from Hassan's African home town. We see Venice and the Venetian characters through Hassan's eyes as portrayed by Hassan's townspeople. In the tradition of Abibigoro, we created a voice for the community that is free to periodically comment on and even disagree with the play's action.

Overcoming Double Consciousness

Once we were in Ghana and working with Abibigromma, having Hassan tell the story of his recent trip to Venice seemed to be the appropriate course of action. This change transferred control of the play's through line from Gratiano to Hassan. Abibigoro stories are often structured with circular plots. The story begins at the end and circles to the beginning and around and back to the end. Storytellers announce they will explain a certain phenomenon such as "how spider obtained the sky god's stories." Since the audience already knows how the story ends, they accept the storyteller as a conveyor of truth, and focus on the story teller's performance. The tradition of Abibigoro also demands that the play move back and forth from narrative to action. Hence, the Abibigromma production contains narrative, singing and dancing as well as dialogue between characters. But even dialogue between characters recognizes the presence of an audience and address that presence.

The Abibigromma version of *Fortunes of The Moor* begins as Hassan returns to his home and tells how things went in Venice. As the production was staged, the audience cannot be certain whether Hassan, Elissa, and Somaia have returned with or without the baby. The community asks if they were successful; to which Hassan replies, "We will tell the story." In the tradition of Abibigoro, the point of view from which the audience observes the story is the point of view of the story teller. The return of Hassan, Elissa, and Somaia to their home becomes the play's enveloping action. The play ends with the same welcoming ceremony except the baby is present. Since we were in residence with Abibigromma for ten weeks, we were able to develop some of the play's new attributes through company participation. For example, we described a scenario

108

for the beginning of the play that involved the return of Hassan, Elissa, and Somaia to their home whereupon we asked, "What kind of welcome would their village provide?" The company created music and dance for the occasion.

The play begins with actors entering the stage and announcing they are going to do a play. They talk about the play's premise and justify its enactment. Hassan, as the Griot, pours a libation to request that the act of storytelling be blessed. He asks the townspeople to portray the characters and help tell the story. As they don their costumes and masks, they sing and dance to bid Hassan and his family a safe journey to Venice. Creating suspense accommodates American (and African American) sensibilities by not not disclosing what happens to the infant. The actors wear African costumes and use African artifacts for props. The play's locale is Hassan's African home town. The play's focus is on Hassan who introduces himself and his family and states his goal. Abibigoro permits, even encourages, Hassan, as his character or as the Griot, to step out of a scene and comment on the action to both the audience and the townspeople. The townspeople, in turn, occasionally comment on the action to the Griot.

PRODUCTION PHOTOGRAPHS

Premiere production, November 30 to December 17, 1995, at the Frank Silvera Writers' Workshop, Garland Thompson, producer, directed by Charles E. Wise.

(L to R), Judith Barnett as Elissa, Todd Davis as Hassan, Kat Walker as Somaia.

Connecticut Repertory Theatre, March 2 to 5, 1997, directed by Allie Woods, Jr., (L to R), C. Mingo Long as Hassan, Aleta Mitchell as Elissa, Deidra LaWan Johnson as Somaia.

Abibigromma [Ghana's National Theatre Company] opened August 15, 1997 with subsequent performances at several venues. The masks worn by the characters on the left were used to designate characters as Venetians.

The African masks were created in a Ghanaian village known for its wood carvers.

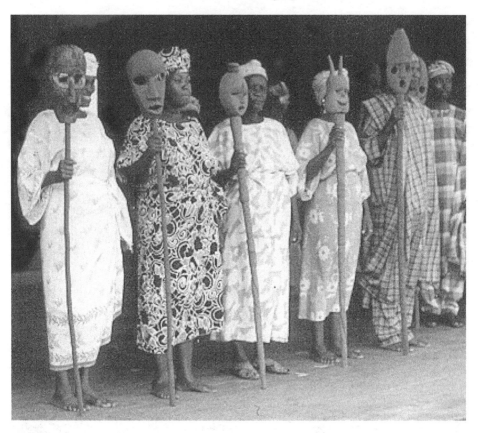

African masks as used in Abibigromma's production, directed by Carlton W. Molette, choreography by Habib Chester Iddrisu, music composed and conducted by Kwisi Brown.

The play opened at the School of Performing Arts, University of Ghana, Legon, August 15 to 17, 1997.

It was later presented at the National Theatre in Accra and the Pan-African Historical Theatre Festival in Cape Coast.

University of Louisville, January 31 to February 11, 2001, directed by Nefertiti Burton, costumes and masks designed by Loyce Arthur.

Ohio State University, February 25 to March 7, 1998, directed by Anthony Hill, achieved contrast between Moors and Venetians with actors who appear racially correct and costumes that evoke historical accuracy. In this early scene, actors who later portray Venetians [without masks] wear African masks and costumes. Designers: Dan Gray, Scenic; Judy Chestnut, Costumes; Robert Johnson, Lighting.

Through most of the Ohio State University production, neither nationality wore masks as in the early scene on the previous page. The three Moors appear as seen here on the left and the three Venetians appear as seen here on the right.

OTHER WORKS BY THE PLAYWRIGHTS

NON-FICTION:
Afrocentric Theatre offers a framework for interpreting, analyzing, and evaluating theatre arts based in Afrocentric culture and values. It updates and expands the Molettes' ground-breaking book, *Black Theatre: Premise and Presentation*, that has been required reading in Black theatre courses for over twenty-five years. Plays, as well as film and video dramas, are not Afrocentric simply because they are by Black playwrights, or have Black characters, or address Black themes or issues. Instead, plays, film and video dramas, are Afrocentric when they embrace and disseminate Afrocentric culture and values.

FULL LENGTH PLAYS:
Doctor B.S. Black– A Farcical Musical [also a non-musical version] loosely based on Moliere's *The Doctor in Spite of Himself.* Begonia punishes her husband for his womanizing ways by convincing naive locals that he can work amazing cures, but only if he is beaten first. Crafty con artist B.S. "confesses" he is a doctor and connives to conceal his inability to actually cure anyone. *One set, 120 minutes. 4 men, 4 women.*

Legacy– Amanda Overton, guardian of the local social hierarchy, has never met her only niece. Justine was born and raised in Paris. Her mother [Amanda's sister] left her southern nest to attend Radcliffe, fell in love and eloped to Paris with a Harvard man. Amanda plans to introduce her legacy to "society" and groom her to be a "refined Southern lady." Justine arrives and Amanda discovers she is Black. *Comedy. Unit set, 125 minutes, 4 women, 1 man.*

Other Works by the Playwrights

***Noah's Ark*–** Published in *Center Stage*, ed. Eileen Ostrow, University of Illinois Press. A professor's son is running a rogue radio station and the government considers him a terrorist. *One set, 120 minutes, 4 women, 3 men.*

***Presidential Timber*–** A television journalist chronicles the financial mess at mythological, historically-Black Pemberton State University putting a strain on her romantic relationship with Pemberton's Vice President for Academic Affairs. The President's audacious plan to obliterate the University's financial woes unravels as Pemberton stumbles along the precipice. *Comedy. Unit set, 90 minutes, 4 men, 2 women.*

***Prudence*–** In 1832 Connecticut, a firestorm of bigotry is unleashed when Prudence Crandall lets a "Colored girl" enroll in her Academy. Organized intimidation causes Crandall to close her school and reopen as an academy for "young ladies and little misses of color." Courage and perseverance initially sustain Prudence and her students, but opposition grows more widespread and violent. *Unit set, 110 minutes, 4 women, 2 men, (most play several characters).*

ONE ACT PLAYS:
***Booji*–** A Black lawyer, to the dismay of his friends and colleagues, mentors a group of young "Black revolutionaries" while one "Black revolutionary" uses the group to conceal criminal activity. *Unit set, 70 minutes, 8 women, 10 men.*

***Our Short Stay*–** Based on the same actual events as *Prudence*, focuses more on the students and less on Prudence. Can be presented without theatrical scenery or lighting. *Unit set, 40 minutes, 2 women, 1 man (all play several characters).*

Rosalee Pritchett – Production rights through Dramatists Play Service. Black women play bridge, discuss aspirations and express relief that the National Guard is "keeping ghetto Blacks from looting and rioting." Then, one of them is raped. *Unit set, 60 minutes, 5 women, 4 men.*

TEN MINUTE PLAYS:
A Fond Farewell – Charlie Burns is dead. His wife and ex-wife do not agree about how Charlie's fond farewell should proceed. Then, Mr. Barber arrives. *3 characters (2 women, 1 man).*

Do You Care Enough? – Three greeting card executives have a mandate to devise a new reason for consumers to purchase cards. *3 characters (1 woman, 2 men).*

The Great Xmas Race – It's the second coming. It's reality television. Each contestant's last name is King. Each is taking a gift to Bethlehem. Fame and fortune await the three Kings who arrive first. But first they must get through the world's busiest airport. *4 characters (2 men, 2 either gender).*

Kin Ship – In 2147, the Racial Identity Determination Bureau investigates an appeal. The Global Union of Nations is populating its newly established Lunar Colony and the twin sister ordered to stay wants to go but the twin ordered to go wants to stay. *3 characters (2 women, 1 either gender).*

Other Works by the Playwrights

Last Supper– The staff at a café in Memphis prepares supper for Dr. Martin Luther King, Jr. on the eve of the historic march in Memphis in support of the sanitation workers. *4 characters (3 women, 1 man).*

Move the Car– A couple married for over twenty-five years has purchased a twenty-eight-year-old car. They hire an auto shop proprietor to refurbish the car and move it into their bedroom. *3 characters (2 men, 1 woman).*

Out of Time– A customer attempts to purchase a watch at a store that advertises used watches; but the proprietor refuses to sell a watch until the customer demonstrates an understanding of what time is. *All 3 characters either gender.*

Silver Tongue– A young politician discovers the secret of the father's political success while aspiring to follow in the father's footsteps. *2 characters (both either gender).*

Tee-shirt History– A novice entrepreneur encounters obstacles while selling souvenirs near Atlanta's Piedmont Park as an event celebrating Dr. Martin Luther King, Jr.'s birthday begins. *3 characters (2 men, 1 either gender).*

Widgets– In 1908, a young newspaper reporter interviews the recently named Employee of the Year at the World Wide Widget Works. *2 characters, both men.*

For permission to produce and royalty information,
visit www.Afrocentrictheatre.com
and click CONTACT THE AUTHOR.

ABOUT THE PLAYWRIGHTS

Barbara and Carlton Molette, 2013 recipients of the National Black Theatre Festival's Living Legend Award and the Ethel Woolson Award for their new play *Legacy*, collaborate on plays, scholarly articles and two books– *Black Theatre: Premise and Presentation*, and *Afrocentric Theatre*. Members of the Dramatists Guild since 1971, their playwrighting collaborations began with *Rosalee Pritchett,* presented by the Negro Ensemble Company, the Free Southern Theatre, several university theatres, published by Dramatists Play Service and in *Black Writers of America*.

A musical, *Dr. B. S. Black*, in collaboration with Charles Mann was produced at Atlanta's Peachtree Playhouse by Theatre of the Stars and Just Us Theatre with Samuel L. Jackson in the title role and later at other theatres in Washington, D. C., Houston, and Memphis. *Fortunes of The Moor* premiered in New York at the Frank Silvera Writers' Workshop and later at over a dozen venues including the National Theatre of Ghana, Chicago's ETA Creative Arts; and universities including Western Michigan, Brown, Ohio State, the Universities of Louisville, Pittsburgh, and Connecticut.

Miami's M Ensemble premiered *Our Short Stay* in 2005. *Prudence* premiered at the Connecticut Repertory Theatre in 2006. Readings of *Presidential Timber* have been presented at the National Black Theatre Festival, New York's New Federal Theatre, by Bowie State University at the Kennedy Center in Washington, and New Life Productions in Columbia, SC. Other full length plays include *Noah's Ark* (published in *Center Stage*), and *Booji*.

About the Playwrights

Premieres of ten minute plays include *Out of Time* at New York's Turtle Productions in 2011; *Move the Car* in 2012 at the Warehouse Performing Arts Center, North Carolina; *Tee Shirt History* at Atlanta's Essential Theatre in 2012; *A Fond Farewell* at Greenbrier Valley Theatre in West Virginia in 2014; both *Last Supper* in 2013 and *Kin Ship* in 2014 at Houston's Fade to Black. Other ten minute plays include *Widgets*, *Silver Tongue*, *Do You Care Enough*, and *The Great Xmas Race*.

Barbara J. Molette (B.A. Florida A. & M. U., M.F.A. Florida State U., Ph.D. U. of Missouri) Professor Emerita, Eastern Connecticut State U.; taught at Spelman College, Texas Southern U., and Baltimore City Community College where she was Director of Writing Across the Curriculum. She was Administrative Fellow, Mid-Missouri Associated Colleges and Universities; Director of Arts-in-Education Programs, Mayor's Advisory Committee on Art and Culture in Baltimore; and English Department Chair, Eastern Connecticut State U.

Carlton W. Molette (B.A. Morehouse College, M.A. U. of Iowa, Ph.D. Florida State U.) Professor Emeritus of Dramatic Arts and African American Studies, U. of Connecticut; taught at Spelman College, Florida A. & M., Howard, Atlanta, and Texas Southern Universities; was Division of Fine Arts Chair, Spelman; School of Communications Dean, Texas Southern; Dean of Arts and Sciences, Lincoln (MO), and Vice President for Academic Affairs, Coppin State (MD).

CPSIA information can be obtained
at www.ICGtesting.com
Printed in the USA
LVHW031753080119
603164LV00004B/553/P